2 I st CENTURY

LIFESKILLS

M A T H E M A T I C S

Everyday Life Math

SADDLEBACK
EDUCATIONAL PUBLISHING
www.sdlback.com

ISBN-13: 978-1-61651-408-2
ISBN-10: 1-61651-408-6
eBook: 978-1-61247-002-3

Printed in the United States of America

16 15 14 13 12   7 8 9 10 11

Table of Contents

Unit 5: Community

Unit 6: Thinking about the Future

Unit 7: Thrifty Thinking

Unit 8: Sustaining the World

To the Student

Welcome to *Everyday Life!* This is Book 1 of the *21st Century Lifeskills Mathematics* series.

The goal of this book and the other books in this series is to build your confidence and practical math skills. You will use these math skills in everyday situations throughout your life.

You solve problems and make mathematical decisions every day. You compare products and make choices about what to buy. You work to earn money. You decide what to spend and how much to save.

21st Century Lifeskills Mathematics gives you strategies to solve everyday math problems in a variety of ways. It strengthens your skills and gives you practice with many different math topics. Each of the six books presents topics you are likely to encounter in everyday life. Each book includes problems that involve estimation, equations, mental math, calculators, and critical thinking. Each book includes additional topic-specific skills such as graphing, averages, statistics, ratios, and measurement.

Each unit begins with a preview lesson, which models and explains the types of problems you will encounter in the unit. Then there are five lessons, at least one of which is usually a game. Each unit ends with a review of the unit concepts. There are illustrations and graphic art throughout.

Here is a list of the titles of the other books in the *21st Century Lifeskills Mathematics* series:
Book 2: Home & School
Book 3: On the Job
Book 4: Budgeting & Banking
Book 5: Smart Shopping
Book 6: Sports, Hobbies, & Recreation

With review and practice, you will build your math skills and learn to approach everyday mathematical situations with confidence! *21st Century Lifeskills Mathematics* will help you become a successful problem solver!

Unit 1 — *Personal Care*

Preview

How You Will Use This Unit

Taking care of yourself involves many different things. Hair care and dental care are just two examples. You probably also buy face and skin products, soaps, and other items. As you compare products and make choices, you will often use math. The math skills you use include mental math and estimation, basic operations, and even equations and statistics.

What You Will Do in This Unit

In this unit, math steps demonstrate how to solve problems. These steps can help you answer questions such as these:

You buy some shampoo and conditioner at the store. How can you quickly estimate the total cost?

Surveys are often used to find out what concerns people. The report of a survey tells you the total number of people who participated. How can you find the number of people in this survey who are concerned about their skin?

Your dental bill comes to $250. How do you check that this is correct?

You write checks to buy items such as sunglasses or other things. How do you keep track of the amount of money you have left in your checking account?

What You Can Learn from This Unit

When you complete this unit, you will have used mathematics to solve problems related to personal care. These problems are similar to those that may actually occur in your daily life.

(Lesson 1)

→ *Hair Care*

Example You buy shampoo, conditioner, gel, a comb, and a brush. Here are the prices of these items:

$$\$3 \quad \$4 \quad \$6 \quad \$2 \quad \$7$$

Use mental math to find the total cost of these items.

Solve

Step 1: Circle a pair of numbers that are easy to add mentally.

$$\textcircled{\$3} \quad \$4 \quad \$6 \quad \$2 \quad \textcircled{\$7}$$

Step 2: Draw a square around another pair of numbers that are easy to add mentally.

$$\textcircled{\$3} \quad \boxed{\$4} \quad \boxed{\$6} \quad \$2 \quad \textcircled{\$7}$$

Answer the Question

Step 3: You pay $22 for the five products.

✎ Now try these problems.

1. Selena buys a hair dryer, hair spray, a hair straightening product, and hair clips. Here are the prices of these items:

$$\$12 \quad \$9 \quad \$8 \quad \$11$$

Mark pairs of prices as you use mental math to find the total cost.

Answer: Selena pays $_____ for the four products.

2. Health club members use about 25 packets of shampoo a day. How many packets of shampoo will club members use in four 7-day weeks?

Think about which way to do this problem is easier:
$25 \times (4 \times 7)$ or $(25 \times 4) \times 7$

Circle the correct answer.

A 25   C 175

B 100   D 700

3. A special sale bottle of Today's Hair contains 10 fluid ounces and costs $9.99. The label on the special bottle says you get 3 more fluid ounces than in a regular bottle, for the same cost.

Draw a line from the list on the left to the list on the right to show a match between the ounces in a regular bottle and the cost of the regular bottle.

Ounces	Cost
13.5	$9.99
10.2	$6.99
7	$12.99

4. Paul buys 16 ounces of *Wow!* hair-spiker styling glue. He shares it with his three brothers. The four boys each use about 1 ounce a week.

Estimate how long the styling glue will last.

Answer: _____

5. Bella takes a bottle of hair color to the checkout counter. Its price tag says $4.89. Bella knows she has to pay a sales tax of 10%.

Circle the smallest bill she can hand to the clerk to cover the total cost.

6. A 12-ounce bottle of *MegaVolume* costs $11.89.

Circle the best estimate of the price per ounce.

    A $0.50   **B** $1   **C** $2   **D** $12

☆ *Challenge Problem*
You may want to talk this one over with a partner.

Teresa wants to have long hair by the start of the summer vacation on June 1. It is now October 1 and her hair is one inch below ear level. Hair grows at about $\frac{1}{2}$ inch per month. Will her hair be 10 inches below ear level by June 1? Explain your answer.

_____

_____

_____

Lesson 2

Example A survey of 1,589 girls showed three out of four are concerned about oily skin. What is a rough estimate of the number of girls concerned about oily skin?

Solve

Step 1: Underline the sentence that tells you the number of girls concerned about oily skin.

In a survey of 1,589 girls, three out of four are concerned about oily skin.

Step 2: Now write the same sentence, using the language of math.

$\frac{3}{4}$ × 1,589 are concerned about oily skin.

Step 3: $\frac{3}{4}$ × 1,589 is the same as $\frac{3 \times 1,589}{4}$.

Think about numbers that would be easy to calculate. Round 1,589 up to 1,600.

$\frac{3 \times 1,600}{4}$ is the same as $\frac{3 \times \overset{400}{\cancel{1,600}}}{\underset{1}{\cancel{4}}}$.

1,200

Answer the Question

Step 4: About 1,200 of the girls surveyed are concerned about oily skin.

4

✏ Now try these problems.

1. Of 2,005 boys who took part in the same survey, one out of two is concerned about oily skin. What is a rough estimate of the number of boys who are concerned about oily skin? Think about rounding 2,005 up to a number that is divisible by 2.

Answer: About _____ boys are concerned about oily skin.

2. Wesley buys a scrub, a cleanser, and a lotion. He gets them gift-packed together for $14.99, including tax. Wesley has $44. Circle the number of gift packs he can buy.

3. The advertisement says, "Buy three products in a straight line and pay only $15.50."

Lotion $5	Pumice $6	Razor $8.50
Dry skin kit $10.50	Bandages $3	Lip gloss $2.25
Face scrub $7	Razor blades $6.50	Eye crayon $4

Mark the three products you could buy that are worth the most.

4. Justin notices that a pack of cartridges lasts four weeks with his *ShaveMate* razor. A pack lasted only one week with his old *RazorSense* razor. A pack of cartridges costs $20. How much money will Justin save in one year (52 weeks) using his *ShaveMate* razor? Circle the correct answer.

A $20　　　　　**C** $780

B $260　　　　　**D** $1,040

Soapy Percents

♟ A Board Game (for Two Players)

The goal of this game is to place six counters in a straight line—horizontally, vertically, or diagonally—on the game board. First, you create a fraction by tossing a number cube. Then you place a counter on the board to show the percent equal to that fraction.

Materials

Game board (on the next page), counters in two colors, one number cube.

Directions

1. Choose a counter color for each player. Sit with players around the game board.

2. Player 1 tosses the number cube. This number is the numerator of the fraction. The same player tosses again to get the denominator. (Make a note of this fraction on a sheet of scratch paper.) Then Player 1 places a counter on the game board in any one of the spaces which show a percent equal to that fraction. Player 2 checks the placement of the counter. If it is not correct, Player 2 gets to choose a correct space and move the counter there.

3. Player 2 then takes a turn doing the same thing, with Player 1 checking.

4. Players alternate turns and placing counters. If all the spaces for that percent are already covered, the player who tossed that fraction misses a turn.

5. The winner is the first player to have six counters in a straight line.

✏ Before you play the game, try these warm-up problems.

1. If you have poison ivy or chickenpox, oatmeal and milk soap can help soothe your skin. The soap package says the ingredients are combined in the ratio 1:2. This ratio is the same as the fraction $\frac{1}{2}$. Put counters in all the space(s) on the game board that show a percent equal to this ratio.

2. In Shannon's middle school, 60% of the students say they use anti-bacterial soap at home. You want to put a counter on the 60% percent space on the game board. What two numbers do you have to get with the number cube?

   Answer: _____ and then _____.

Game Board for *Soapy Percents*

Numerator

Denominator	1	2	3	4	5	6
1	100%	200%	300%	400%	500%	600%
2	50%	100%	150%	200%	250%	300%
3	33.3%	66.7%	100%	133.3%	166.7%	200%
4	25%	50%	75%	100%	125%	150%
5	20%	40%	60%	80%	100%	120%
6	16.7%	33.3%	50%	66.7%	83.3%	100%

Lesson 4

→ *Dental Care*

Example The total on Monika's dental bill reads $310.

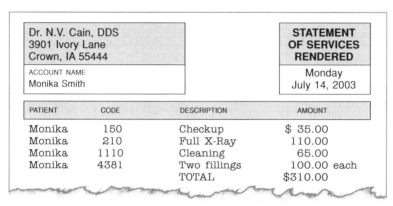

Is this bill correct? What error was made by the person who wrote the bill?

Solve

Step 1: Write the expression and find the total dollar amount for the items on the bill. (Remember that Monika had two fillings.)

$35 + $110 + $65 + ($100 × 2) = $410

Step 2: Compare your total to the total on the bill.

$410 ≠ $310

Answer the Question

Step 3: The bill is not correct. The charge is for only one filling, not two.

✎ Now try these problems.

1. Earl has a checkup, a cleaning, and one filling. The clerk itemizes his bill. Fill in the total.

Checkup:	$ 35
Cleaning	$ 65
Filling:	$100
Total:	_____

2. Chelsea's insurance plan pays 20% of all dental costs. Chelsea has a checkup that costs $35, two fillings that cost $100 each, and a root canal that costs $665. How much will Chelsea have to pay after the insurance plan has paid its part? Circle the correct answer.

A $180   **B** $450   **C** $720   **D** $900

3. The health food store advertises parsley as a natural breath freshener. A bottle of mouthwash costs $2.39 and lasts two weeks. A bunch of parsley costs $0.95 and lasts a week. Which is the most economical way to freshen your breath? What are the savings?

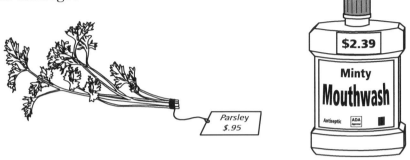

Answer: _____

4. The *OnLineDentist* advertises products to give you brighter whiter teeth in seven days without a dental visit. Jake ordered enough products to try them for seven days. Jake's total bill is $81.62, including 6% sales tax.

a. Circle the amount on the bill that shows the price before sales tax.

b. Draw a square around the amount of the sales tax.

c. Write the cost per day of these products (before tax) at the bottom of the bill.

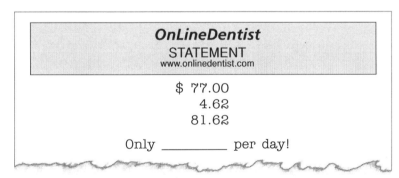

☆ *Challenge Problem*
You may want to talk this one over with a partner.

The dental office offers a 10% discount on the price of its dental products. Sales tax is 8%. Should you calculate the discount *before* or *after* you add the tax? Explain your answer.

_____

_____

Example Lyndon buys tinted sunglasses at *SunGlassesGalore* for $16.29, including sales tax. Complete the check and check stub that Lyndon has started to write. After this purchase, how much does Lyndon have left in his checking account?

CHECK NUMBER: _____	LYNDON WILLIS 289 Beach Lane Magnolia, TX 78884		**435**
DATE: _____			DATE_____
TO: _____	PAY TO THE ORDER OF *SunGlassesGalore*	$	
AMOUNT OF THIS CHECK: _____			
FOR: _____			DOLLARS
BALANCE BROUGHT FORWARD: *$254.50*	**Mission Bank** P.O. Box 444 Magnolia, TX 78884		
BALANCE CARRIED FORWARD: _____	memo _____		
	|: 111000341|: 2589406821||2940		

Solve

Step 1: On the check:
   a. Write the amount of the bill, $16.29, in the check space beginning "$."
   b. Write "Sixteen and $\frac{29}{100}$" on the check line ending "Dollars."
   c. Sign and date the check.

Step 2: On the check stub:
   a. Enter $16.29 in "Amount of this check."
   b. Subtract $16.29 from the "Balance brought forward," and enter the difference in the "Balance carried forward" space.
   c. Enter *SunGlassesGalore,* "tinted sun glasses," date, and check number.

Step 3: On the next check stub: Enter the "Balance carried forward" from the previous check in the "Balance brought forward" space.

Answer the Question

Step 3: Lyndon has $238.21 left in his checking account after this purchase.

✏ Now try these problems.

1. Lyndon has $238.21 in his checking account. He buys one box of 30 *FreshVue* daily contact lenses for $18.60, plus 10% sales tax. After his purchase, what should he write in the "Balance carried forward" space on the check stub?

   Answer: $_____

2. SaraBeth's "balance brought forward" shows she has $175 in her checking account. She writes a deposit slip to deposit $350, and a check to withdraw $150. After these two transactions, what should she should write in the "balance carried forward" space? Circle the amount.

    A $25   **B** $200   **C** $375   **D** $525

3. A customer who buys five sets of earrings gets a free earring stand. Leigh chooses five sets of earrings that cost $8.75 each, before the 10% sales tax. Leigh has $45 in her checking account.

Read the questions in the table below. Then circle the row that shows the correct pair of answers.

Does Leigh have enough money in her account to write a check for the total amount?	Can Leigh get a free earring stand?
Yes	Yes
Yes	No
No	Yes
No	No

4. For *World Peace Day,* the local youth club bought 135 *Peace Day* tote bags. The club members planned to give the bags to the first 135 people who made donations. The bags cost the club $200. They also spent $35 on snacks, and $50 on a youth band (which the band donated back to the club afterward). The club raised $852.50 in donations. After expenses, how much money did the club make? Circle the correct amount.

$567.50 $617.50 $652.50 $852.50 $902.50

☆ *Challenge Problem*
You may want to talk this one over with a partner.

SportsAreIn is giving away a pair of sneakers with each purchase of $50 or more. In the first hour, they gave away 93 free pairs of sneakers, and sold $6,143 worth of goods. To find how much money the store took in on purchases *not* earning free sneakers, what additional information do you need?

Unit 1

Review

Review What You Learned

In this unit you have used mathematics to solve many problems. You have used mental math and estimation, practiced basic operations, and solved equations.

These two pages give you a chance to review the mathematics you used and check your skills.

✔ Check Your Skills

1. You buy hair color, shampoo, hair spray, and a teasing brush. Below are the prices. Use mental math to find how much these items cost altogether.

   $6.50 $5.00 $5.50 $3.50

   Answer: _____

   If you need to review, return to lesson 1 (page 2).

2. In a survey of 2,097 students, three out of five say they are delighted with the results of a new skin cream. What is a rough estimate of the number of students who are delighted with the new skin cream?

   Circle the best answer.

   700   1,200   1,254   1,260

   If you need to review, return to lesson 2 (page 4).

3. The wrapper on the bath treatment product makes a claim. It says the two most important ingredients are combined in a ratio of 2 to 3. What percent is the first ingredient of the second?

   Answer: _____

   If you need to review, return to lesson 3 (page 6).

4. In health class, 40% of the students say they use aloe-enriched face soap at home. Pick one number from each row to make a fraction that is equivalent to 40%.

1	2	3	4	5	6	7	8	9	10
1	2	3	4	5	6	7	8	9	10

   If you need to review, return to lesson 3 (page 6).

12

5. The total on Tony's dental bill is $420.

Dr. N.V. Cain, DDS 3901 Ivory Lane Crown, IA 55444			STATEMENT OF SERVICES RENDERED
ACCOUNT NAME Tony Jones			Wednesday July 30, 2003

PATIENT	CODE	DESCRIPTION	AMOUNT
Tony	150	Checkup	$ 45.00
Tony	210	Full X-Ray	120.00
Tony	1110	Cleaning	55.00
Tony	4381	Two fillings	100.00 each
		TOTAL	$420.00

After his insurance plan pays 25% of the bill, how much will Tony have to pay?

Answer: _____

If you need to review, return to lesson 4 (page 8).

6. Canda has $255.75 in her checking account. She buys a *SchoolCool* bag for $21.00, plus 10% sales tax. Circle the amount of money she will have in her account *after* her purchase.

    A $232.65   **B** $234.75   **C** $255.75   **D** $278.85

If you need to review, return to lesson 5 (page 10).

Write Your Own Problem ✍

Choose a problem you liked from this unit. Write a similar problem using a situation and related facts from your own life. With a partner, share and solve these problems together. Discuss the mathematics and compare the steps you used. If you need to, rewrite or correct the problems. Write your edited problem and the answer here.

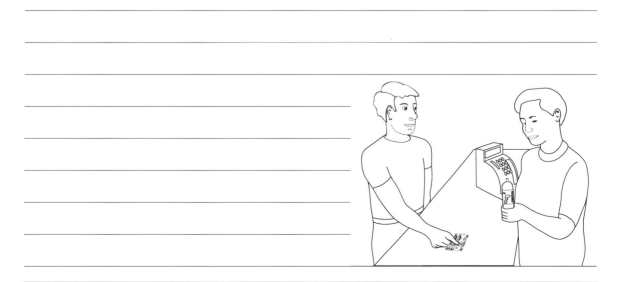

Preview

How You Will Use This Unit

Taking care of your health means watching what you eat, getting exercise, and using medication wisely. Often you can find the information you need in nutrition, calorie, and other health-related charts. Mathematics can help you read charts. The math skills you use include mental math and estimation, basic operations, equations, and statistics.

What You Will Do in This Unit

In this unit, math steps demonstrate how to solve problems. These steps can help you answer questions such as these:

You look at the nutrition chart on a box of cereal. What does the chart tell you about the dietary fiber you will get from one serving? How much of the recommended daily value for fiber is in one serving?

You have a muffin and a glass of milk for a snack. How many calories are in this snack?

You are going on vacation. Will your bottle of medication last until you get home? Do you need to pack a second bottle?

You have been running one hour at lunchtime for three days a week. Now you have to shorten the time you run at lunch. However, you want to keep running the same distance each week. So how many days a week must you run now?

What You Can Learn from This Unit

When you complete this unit, you will have used mathematics to solve problems related to health. These problems are similar to those that may actually occur in your daily life.

14

Example The nutrition chart on a box of JoLeta's favorite cereal says one serving contains 9.5 grams of dietary fiber. This is 38% of the recommended daily value of dietary fiber. What is the recommended daily value of dietary fiber?

Nutrition Facts
Serving Size: 1 cup (55 g)
Servings per box: 7

Amount Per Serving	% Daily Value
Total Fat 3 g	5%
Saturated Fat 0 g	0%
Cholesterol 0 mg	0%
Sodium 240 mg	10%
Total Carbohydrate 36 g	12%
Dietary Fiber 9.5 g	38%
Sugars 9 g	
Protein 8 g	

Solve

Step 1: Use g for the number of grams in the recommended daily value of dietary fiber. The value of g will be the answer to the question. Use g to write a simple sentence that tells how 9.5 grams and 38% are related.

38% of g grams equals 9.5 grams.

Step 2: Now write the same sentence, using the language of math. Write 38% as the equivalent fraction, using a denominator of 100.

$$\frac{38}{100} \times g = 9.5$$

Step 3: To solve this equation, undo what has been done to g. You undo multiplying by $\frac{38}{100}$ by dividing by $\frac{38}{100}$, or multiplying by the reciprocal, $\frac{100}{38}$.

$$g = 9.5 \times \frac{100}{38}$$
$$g = 25$$

Answer the Question

Step 4: The recommended daily value of dietary fiber is 25 grams.

✏ Now try these problems.

1. The chart on a cereal box shows that one serving contains 36 grams of carbohydrates. The chart also lists this as 12% of the

recommended daily value (RDV). What is the recommended daily value of carbohydrates?

Answer: The recommended daily value of carbohydrates is _____ grams.

2. The label on a bottle of cranberry juice shows that one serving provides 4% of the RDV (recommended daily value) for iron. Carlos knows that the recommended daily value of iron for an adult is 18 milligrams. How many milligrams of iron does one serving of this cranberry juice provide?

A 0.22 mg   **B** 0.45 mg   **C** 0.72 mg   **D** 4.5 mg

3. The nutrition chart on the back of a frozen pizza package lists the contents. The chart shows that the pizza contains 39% carbohydrates, 15% protein, 10% fat, and 1% minerals. The rest is water. On the pie chart, write the percents that each ingredient contributes to the whole pizza.

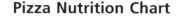

Pizza Nutrition Chart

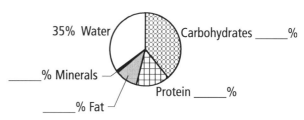

35% Water

Carbohydrates _____ %

_____ % Minerals

_____ % Fat

Protein _____ %

4. Botanists have classified about 24,000 species of plants. However, just 11 species of plants provide 80% of the food for the world.

   a. What part of the plant species provides 80% of the food for the world? Circle the fraction that shows the best estimate.

   $\dfrac{1}{24,000}$ $\dfrac{1}{2,400}$ $\dfrac{1}{240}$ $\dfrac{239}{240}$ $\dfrac{2,399}{2,400}$

   b. What percent of the 24,000 species are *not* included in those that provide most of the food? Draw a square around this percent.

   0.0458%   4.58%   9.995%   99.95%   999.5%

☆ *Challenge Problem*
You may want to talk this one over with a partner.

Every day the World Food Program provides lunch for 15 million children in 60 countries. The cost of a meal is $0.75 per child. A local club collects $551.25 for this program. The contribution from this club will provide lunch for how many children?

Answer: The club will provide lunch for _____ children.

♠ A Card Game (for Two or More Players)

The goal of this game is to build a balanced meal that has a certain number of calories. A balanced meal for this diet contains food from each of the six food lists. Each game begins when the dealer names a target number of calories. First, you evaluate your cards. Then, you pick up and discard cards until you have a balanced meal. The total calories in the meal cannot be more than the target number. Some foods may be on more than one list.

Materials

A deck that has six suits with 12 cards each. You can make these cards from the chart on the next page. Each suit represents one food list. The six food lists are starches, fruit, milk products, fats, vegetables, and meats. Each card tells the number of calories for that food.

Directions

1. One player shuffles the deck of cards. Then each player picks 2 cards. The player with the lowest total number of calories becomes the dealer.

2. The dealer names the target number of calories. Players build meals with their cards to come as close as they can to that target total.

3. The dealer deals 10 cards to each player. The remaining cards are set face down in a stack in the middle. The dealer takes the top card of this stack and turns it face up to start another pile. This is the discard pile.

4. The dealer picks one card either off the face-down stack or from the top of the discard pile. Then the dealer discards one card, so there are still 10. Keep cards that build a balanced meal with total calories less than the target calorie count.

5. Each player then takes a turn (as in step 4). When all cards on the face-down pile are gone, the discard pile replaces it. Turn the pile face down. Then turn the top card face up to start a new discard pile.

6. Continue until one player decides that he or she has the best possible meal. Players then lay their hands down and compare their meals. Any meal that wins must be equal to or less than the calorie count. Players must agree any winning meal is close to a balanced meal. There can be two or more winners if the calorie counts are close.

✎ **Before you play the game, try these warm-up problems.**

1. A 50-gram serving of lettuce contains about 10 calories, but 50 grams of peanuts contains about 325 calories. How many grams of lettuce would you have to eat to get 325 calories?

   Answer: _____

2. Pat ate a watermelon slice (65 calories), a muffin (190 calories), and yogurt (250 calories). What part of a 2,000-calorie daily allowance did Pat eat? Circle the best estimate.

   $\frac{1}{10}$ $\frac{1}{5}$ $\frac{1}{4}$ $\frac{1}{3}$ $\frac{1}{2}$

Cards for *Calories Count*

Starch	Fruit	Milk Products	Fats	Vegetables	Meats
Bagel: 160	Apple: 90	1 cup 1% Milk: 100	Avocado: 360	50 g Lettuce: 10	6 oz Beef: 450
1 Muffin: 190	Banana: 60	1 cup Yogurt: 250	8 Black Olives: 45	Bean Sprouts: 25	4 oz Pork: 400
3 Waffles: 250	$\frac{1}{4}$ Cantaloupe: 40	1 cup Cottage Cheese: 80	10 Green Olives: 45	Spinach: 30	6 oz Chicken: 420
1 cup Cereal: 250	Fruit Cocktail: 110	1 cup Evaporated Milk: 300	50 g Peanut Butter: 325	Carrots: 40	2 Eggs: 150
$\frac{1}{2}$ cup Granola: 160	Grapefruit: 120	3 oz Cheese: 340	10 Pecans: 225	Cucumber: 15	3 oz Sausage: 300
1 cup Grits: 160	Orange: 90	1 cup Soy Milk: 75	handful Mixed Nuts: 280	Tomato: 25	10 oz Spare Ribs: 1,000
2 cups Pasta: 320	6 Prunes: 140	$\frac{1}{2}$ cup Half-and-Half: 250	2 tsp Oil: 90	Squash: 30	Hot Dog: 100
1 cup Rice: 240	$\frac{1}{2}$ cup Raisins: 260	2 Tbsp Sour Cream: 45	3 Tbsp Sesame Seeds: 135	Broccoli: 30	50 g Peanut Butter: 325
Corn on Cob: 160	1 slice Watermelon: 65	1 oz Cream Cheese: 95	2 tsp Butter: 90	Celery: 15	8 oz Fish: 600
2 baked Potatoes: 220	1 cup Apple Juice: 140	2 tsp Whipped Butter: 45	1 tsp Mayonnaise: 45	Corn on Cob: 160	2 oz Salami: 200
1 Pretzel: 80	1 cup Cranberry Juice: 180	2 tsp Butter: 90	3 tsp Margarine: 135	Mushrooms: 25	6 slices Bacon: 300
12 Crackers: 150	1 cup Orange Juice: 120	3 tsp Margarine: 135	2 Tbsp Salad Dressing: 90	Onions: 35	4 oz Tofu: 75

(Lesson 3)

Example Karyn takes garlic because she read an article claiming that it helps to build immunity. The directions give a dosage of 2 tablets 3 times a day. Karyn has already used 36 tablets. There were 120 tablets in the bottle when it was full. In how many days will Karyn need a new bottle?

Solve

Step 1: Subtract the number of tablets Karyn has already used from the number in a full bottle. The result is the number of tablets she has left.

120 – 36 = 84   Karyn has 84 tablets left.

Step 2: Multiply 2 tablets by 3 times a day. This number is how many tablets Karyn takes in one day.

2 × 3 = 6   Karyn takes 6 tablets in one day.

Step 3: Divide the number of tablets left in the bottle by the tablets per day.

84 ÷ 6 = 14   Karyn has 14 daily doses left in the bottle.

Answer the Question

Step 4: Karyn will need a new bottle in 14 days.

✐ Now try these problems.

1. The directions on the package of iron tablets give a dosage of 1 tablet twice a day. Xavier has already used 14 tablets. There were 48 tablets in the package when it was full. In how many days will Xavier need a new package?

Answer: Xavier will need a new package of iron tablets in _____ days.

2. The directions on the antacid bottle say that adults and children over 12 years of age can take two gelcaps every four hours, as needed. Write the equation that shows the number of gelcaps a person can take in 12 hours.

$$2 \times \underline{\hspace{2cm}} = \underline{\hspace{2cm}}$$

3. Directions on the bottle of children's aspirin tell how many tablets can be given to a child.

Age (years)	Weight (lbs)	Dosage
2 to under 4	22 to 35	2 tablets
4 to under 6	36 to 45	3 tablets
6 to under 9	46 to 65	4 tablets
9 to under 11	66 to 76	4 to 5 tablets
11 to under 12	77 to 83	4 to 6 tablets
Children 12 and over		5 to 8 tablets

Samantha's daughter, Stana, is $4\frac{1}{2}$ years old and weighs 36 lbs. How many aspirin tablets can Samantha give Stana to relieve Stana's headache?

A 2 **B** 3 **C** 4 **D** 5

4. The magazine article names grape-seed extract as an antioxidant. The article recommends taking 75 mg three times a day. John finds grape-seed extract in 100 mg capsules. How many capsules should he take over 4 days to keep an average of the recommended dosage? Circle the total number of capsules he should take over 4 days.

☆ *Challenge Problem*
You may want to talk this one over with a partner.

Of 2,000 patients, 1,500 received a new medicine. The rest received a placebo (which has no active ingredients). Of those given the new medicine, 800 said their condition improved. Of the others, 50 who received the placebo said they felt better. Would you say the medicine was effective? Give the reasons that support your position.

_____

_____

_____

→ *Getting Exercise, Staying Fit*

Example Gary swims for one hour three days a week. He decides to shorten his swim time to $\frac{3}{4}$ of an hour. How many days each week will he now swim to keep the same total hours per week?

Solve

Step 1: To find the total time Gary swims each week, multiply one hour by 3.

$1 \times 3 = 3$ Gary swims for 3 hours each week.

Step 2: Find the words that tell about Gary's new, shorter swim time. Underline them.

He decides to shorten his swim time to $\frac{3}{4}$ of an hour.

Step 3: How many days will he swim $\frac{3}{4}$ of an hour to keep a total of 3 hours? Divide the total time by $\frac{3}{4}$ hour to find the number of days.

$3 \div \frac{3}{4} = 3 \times \frac{4}{3}$

$= 4$ On 4 days, he swims $\frac{3}{4}$ hour each day.

Answer the Question

Step 4: Gary swims 4 times a week to maintain the same total swim time per week.

✐ Now try these problems.

1. Trisha runs for 30 minutes six days a week. She decides to extend her daily time to 45 minutes. How many times will she run in one week to keep the same total time per week?

   Answer: Trisha must run _____ times a week to maintain the same total time per week.

2. After the fitness class, Silas takes his pulse for 10 seconds. He counts 24 heartbeats in that time. Circle the number on the chart that shows his rate per minute.

10-sec pulse	10	12	14	16	18	20	22	24	26
Rate per min	60	72	84	96	108	120	132	144	156

3. Meghan does high-impact aerobics for $\frac{3}{4}$ hour in a class. High-impact aerobics burns about 10 calories/hour/kilogram of body mass. Meghan has a body mass of about 55 kilograms. How many calories does Meghan burn by doing her aerobics in the class?

A 0.14   C 412.50

B 0.24   D 733.00

4. Curtis runs 4 laps in the time it takes Webb to run 3 laps. How many laps will Curtis run while Webb runs 9 laps? Use a **W** to show Webb's 9 laps. Use a **C** to show Curtis' laps. The pattern is started for you. Who runs the greater distance, and by how much?

W C   W C   W C   C

Answer: _____

5. Jay and Linda walk together for about $1\frac{1}{2}$ hours on each of 4 days per week. How many hours do they walk each week?

Answer: _____

☆ *Challenge Problem*
You may want to talk this one over with a partner.

Trey is learning a new breathing technique for relaxation. These are the steps:

1. Take a deep breath.
2. Contract the abdominal muscles.
3. Force the breath out through the nose.
4. Release the abdominal muscles.
5. Allow a full breath to expand the lungs.
6. Repeat the exercise, from step 2, 20 times.

Trey wonders how long the exercise will take. What does he need to know to find the answer?

_____

_____

_____

_____

Lesson 5

Vitamin Power

Example A box holds small tubs of fruit yogurt. The tubs are stacked in rows of 6, arranged 5 deep and 4 high.

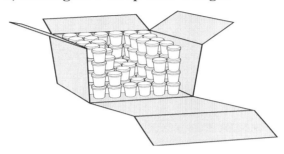

Each small tub contains 25% of the Recommended Dietary Allowance (RDA) of vitamin D. In order for Ruben to get 100% of the RDA (Recommended Dietary Allowance) of vitamin D from the fruit yogurt, how many tubs would he have to eat in a day? How many people could get 100% of their RDA from one box?

Solve

Step 1: Find the number of tubs in the carton.

$6 \times 5 \times 4 = 120$ There are 180 tubs in one box.

Step 2: To find the number of tubs that contain 100% of the RDA, divide 100% by 25%.

$100\% \div 25\% = 4$ Four tubs together contain a total of 100% of the RDA.

Step 3: To find how many people could get 100% from one box, divide the number of tubs by 4.

$180 \div 4 = 30$ Thirty people could get 100% of the RDA from one box.

Answer the Question

Step 4: Ruben would have to eat 4 tubs of fruit yogurt a day to get 100% of the RDA. One box of fruit yogurt will serve 30 people 100% of the RDA.

✏ Now try these problems.

1. Each vitamin C tablet in a bottle contains 25% of the RDA. The bottle contains 300 tablets. If you take enough tablets to get 100% of the RDA each day, how long will the bottle last?

   Answer: The bottle will last _____ days.

2. One serving of 1% milk contains 30% of the RDA of calcium. LuAnne had one serving at breakfast and another serving at lunch. How many more servings will give her 100% of the RDA of calcium?

A $1\frac{1}{3}$ servings   **C** $2\frac{1}{3}$ servings

B 2 servings   **D** 3 servings

3. Marc adds up the amount of food-based vitamin A that he has consumed today. His total so far is 40% of the recommended daily value. To that he adds his daily multivitamin tablet that contains 45% of the RDA of vitamin A. Circle the food that will bring Marc's total for the day up to 100% of the RDA of vitamin A.

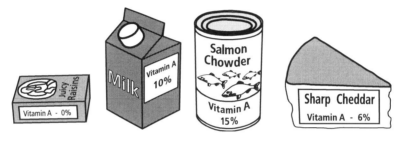

4. Beverly shares a box of raisins equally with her two friends. How do you find the average number of raisins they each get?

Answer: _____

☆ *Challenge Problem*
You may want to talk this one over with a partner.

Natural vitamin E softgels are on sale today for 30% off the regular price. Last month Hal paid the regular price, $9, for a bottle of the same product. Today he buys two bottles at the sale price. He says that the average price he will have paid for all three bottles will be only $7.20 per bottle. Is he right or wrong? Explain your answer.

_____

_____

_____

_____

Review

Review What You Learned

In this unit you have used mathematics to solve many problems. You have used mental math and estimation, practiced basic operations, solved equations, and used statistics.

These two pages give you a chance to review the mathematics you used and check your skills.

✔ Check Your Skills

1. The chart on a cereal box shows that one serving contains 32% of the RDA for dietary fiber. The RDA for dietary fiber is 25 grams. Write in the box on the chart the number of grams of dietary fiber in one serving.

Nutrition Facts
Serving Size: 1 cup (55 g)
Servings per box: 8

Amount Per Serving	% Daily Value
Total Fat 3 g	5%
Saturated Fat 0 g	0%
Cholesterol 0 mg	0%
Sodium 220 mg	10%
Total Carbohydrate 36 g	12%
Dietary Fiber ☐ g	32%
Sugars 12 g	
Protein 7 g	

If you need to review, return to lesson 1 (page 15).

2. One slice of bread contains 60 calories. How many slices of bread would you need to eat to consume 360 calories?

   A 3   **C** 10

   B 6   **D** 30

   If you need to review, return to lesson 2 (page 17).

3. To make one dose, Chispa puts 2 drops of a herbal remedy into a 30 ml bottle and adds spring water. He has now used 54 drops of the 120 that the full bottle contained. How many more times can Chispa use his herbal remedy?

   Answer: _____

   If you need to review, return to lesson 3 (page 19).

4. Darien studies this chart showing the rate of calories burned for certain activities. The rates give the calories/hour/kilogram of body mass.

Sleeping	Bathing, dressing	Walking quickly	Light aerobics	Running, swimming
1.1	3.1	4.4	8.2	10.5

Darien looks at the rate for an hour of light aerobics followed by a one-hour quick walk. She decides she will burn more calories with an hour of running or swimming followed by an hour of sleeping. Is she correct? What is the difference in the rates for her two plans?

Answer: _____

If you need to review, return to lesson 3 (page 19).

5. Kit used to run one hour at lunchtime on four days of the week. His work schedule changed so that now he has only 40 minutes per day to run. Circle the number of times Kit must run in one week to maintain the same total time.

1   2   3   4   5   6   7

If you need to review, return to lesson 4 (page 21).

Write Your Own Problem

Choose a problem you liked from this unit. Write a similar problem using a situation and related facts from your life. With a partner, share and solve these problems together. Discuss the mathematics and compare the steps you used. If you need to, rewrite or correct the problems. Write your edited problem and the answer here.

_____

_____

_____

_____

_____

_____

Unit 3

Getting Around

Preview

How You Will Use This Unit

You do many different things as part of getting around in your neighborhood, town, or state. You may calculate how long a trip will take. You may interpret data from charts of bus or train schedules. You may also calculate the cost of gas for a car trip. As you compare figures and make decisions, you will often use math. The math skills you use include mental math and estimation, basic operations and equations, and statistics.

What You Will Do in This Unit

In this unit, math steps demonstrate how to solve problems. These steps can help you answer questions such as these.

The local bus makes a round trip several times a day. What time should you catch the bus at one stop to get to another stop by a certain time?

You are comparing bicycles in the store, and the sales person talks about "gear advantage." What does this mean?

You decide to walk instead of taking the bus. Will you still get to your destination on time?

How far is your campsite by car from the camp entrance?

You have a long trip to make and want to keep your costs to a minimum. How can you compare the cost of gas and the time for the trip, using different average speeds?

What You Can Learn from This Unit

When you complete this unit, you will have used mathematics to solve problems related to getting around. These problems are similar to those that may actually occur in your daily life.

Example

Bus 2A Schedule

Pioneer Village	8:00 a.m.	9:00 a.m.	10:00 a.m.	—	—	1:00 p.m.	—	3:00 p.m.
Airport	8:10 a.m.	9:10 a.m.	10:10 a.m.	—	—	—	2:10 p.m.	3:10 p.m.
South Beach	8:20 a.m.	—	10:20 a.m.	—	12:20 p.m.	—	2:20 p.m.	—
Town Center	8:30 a.m.	9:30 a.m.	10:30 a.m.	11:30 a.m.	12:30 p.m.	1:30 p.m.	2:30 p.m.	3:30 p.m.
Heritage Park	8:35 a.m.	—	10:35 a.m.	11:35 a.m.	12:35 p.m.	1:35 p.m.	—	3:35 p.m.
Ferry Landing	8:45 a.m.	9:45 a.m.	10:45 a.m.	—	12:45 p.m.	1:45 p.m.	2:45 p.m.	3:45 p.m.
North Beach Artist Colony	—	—	11:00 a.m.	12:00 noon	—	2:00 p.m.	—	4:00 p.m.

Bus 2A makes round trips through the town every day. The bus stops at each place just long enough for the people to get off and on. A blank line indicates that the bus does not stop to take on or let off passengers. Johnna decides to see the town by bus, starting at the Town Center. How long will it take her to make the round trip?

Solve

Step 1: Find the row that shows when the bus leaves the Town Center. Underline or highlight the entries in this row.

Town Center	8:30 a.m.	9:30 a.m.	10:30 a.m.	11:30 a.m.	12:30 p.m.	1:30 p.m.	2:30 p.m.	3:30 p.m.

Step 2: Read the times across row 4. What is the pattern? How long is it from one trip until the bus is back at the Town Center for the next? To find the time for a round trip, subtract one time from the next.

9:30 a.m. – 8:30 a.m. = 1:00 hour

Answer the Question

Step 3: It will take Johnna 1 hour to make the round trip.

✏ Now try these problems.

Use the schedule for the 2A bus.

1. Denny is staying at Pioneer Village. He decides to make a round trip of the town, taking the 9 a.m. bus. What time will he get back to Pioneer Village? Circle his return time on this row of the schedule.

| Pioneer Village | 8:00 a.m. | 9:00 a.m. | 10:00 a.m. | — | — | 1:00 p.m. | — | 3:00 p.m. |

2. Skip and his friends are staying at South Beach. How often can they take a bus to the Town Center?

    A every half hour   **C** every hour and a half

    B every hour   **D** every two hours

3. McIntosh and Associates have a meeting at the city hall in the Town Center at 12 noon. They will fly into the airport and then take the bus to town. What is the latest they can be at the airport bus stop to get a bus for their meeting?

Answer: _____

4. Francelle works until 2:00 p.m. each day at *PegLeg's Oyster Bar,* which is close to the ferry landing. Circle the first bus that she can take to get to North Beach Artist Colony by 4:00 p.m.

5. The garden club decides to have a planning meeting in Heritage Park. They catch the 10:30 a.m. bus from the Town Center. They miss the 12:35 p.m. bus back. They decide to wait for the next bus. How long will they spend in the park?

Answer: _____

☆ *Challenge Problem*
You may want to talk this one over with a partner.

The cousins leave their car at the Town Center parking lot at 9:00 a.m. The parking fee is $0.25/half hour. They catch the 9:30 a.m. bus to South Beach where they sunbath for two hours. Then they catch the bus to Heritage Park and spend an hour wandering around the gardens. From there they catch the bus to the North Beach Artist Colony to spend at least 30 minutes. The bus from there stops at the Town Center every hour on the half hour. The bus goes out of service at 5 p.m. What is the earliest they can get back to the Town Center? How much will their parking fee be?

_____

_____

_____

Example

Brooke is checking her bicycle. First, she turns the pedals once and counts how many times this makes the wheel turn. Then she makes a chart of the number of wheel revolutions and pedal revolutions.

Wheel Revolutions	3.5	7	10.5	14	17.5
Pedal Revolutions	2	4	6	8	10

Next, she counts the number of teeth on both the wheel gear and the pedal gear. The ratio of teeth on the pedal gear to teeth on the wheel gear (the "gear advantage") is 1.75. How does the ratio of wheel revolutions to pedal revolutions compare with the gear advantage?

Solve

Step 1: Find the ratio of the number of wheel revolutions to pedal revolutions: Pick one pair of numbers from the chart, for example 7:4. Write this ratio as a fraction and then as a decimal.

$\frac{7}{4} = 1.75$

Step 2: Check other pairs of numbers from the chart to see if the ratio is the same.

$\frac{3.5}{2} = 1.75$ $\qquad$ $\frac{10.5}{6} = 1.75$ $\qquad$ $\frac{14}{8} = 1.75$ $\qquad$ $\frac{17.5}{10} = 1.75$

Step 3: Compare this common ratio to the gear advantage, 1.75.

1.75 = 1.75. They are equal.

Answer the Question

Step 4: The ratio of the number of wheel revolutions to pedal revolutions is equal to the gear advantage.

✏️ Now try these problems.

1. Vijay counts the number of wheel revolutions for six pedal revolutions. Complete the chart with the number of wheel revolutions for each number of pedal revolutions.

Wheel Revolutions			9.6		
Pedal Revolutions	2	4	6	8	10

2. The gear advantage on Simone's bicycle is 2.5. How many pedal revolutions will her bicycle make to get 30 wheel revolutions?

A 12   **B** 14.5   **C** 27.5   **D** 75

3. The gear advantage on Myron's bicycle is 2.5. He can pedal at about 50 pedal revolutions per minute. How many wheel revolutions per minute is this? The circumference of the wheel tires on his bike measures 81 inches. How many inches can Myron travel in one minute? . . . how many feet?

Answers: _____ revolutions; _____ inches; _____ feet

4. Cass buys Myron's bicycle (see #3: gear advantage = 2.5 and circumference = 81 in.). Cass changes the gearing so that the gear advantage is now 3.0. Cass and Myron both pedal at the same rate (50 revolutions per minute). How many *more* feet can Cass travel in one minute than Myron could? Circle the correct answer.

1.4 feet   10.12 feet   168.75 feet   1,012.5 feet

☆ *Challenge Problem*
You may want to talk this one over with a partner.

A certain bicycle has 19 teeth on the wheel gear and 30 teeth on the pedal gear. The circumference of the wheel tires measures 85 inches.

a. How many *feet* could you travel on this bicycle in 100 wheel revolutions?

b. How many *wheel* revolutions would it take to travel one mile? (One mile = 5,280 feet.)

c. At 50 *pedal* revolutions a minute, how many minutes would it take to travel one mile?

a. _____ feet;   **b.** _____ wheel revolutions;   **c.** _____ minutes

---

Lesson 3

Example Alex walks the 1.5 miles to school whenever he misses the 7:30 a.m. bus. The walk takes him 25 minutes. School starts at 8 a.m. On Wednesday he leaves home 5 minutes after the bus has passed. How late will he be for school?

Solve

Step 1: Draw a number line and mark 5-minute intervals on it, from 7:30 a.m. to 8:30 a.m.

7:30 a.m.   8:00 a.m.   8:30 a.m.

○ ○ ○ ○ ○ ○ ○ ○ ○ ○ ○ ○ ○

Step 2: Shade the mark on the number line that is 5 minutes after the bus has passed.

7:30 a.m.   8:00 a.m.   8:30 a.m.

○ ● ○ ○ ○ ○ ○ ○ ○ ○ ○ ○ ○

Step 3: Count 25 minutes on the number line from the shaded mark. Shade that mark.

7:30 a.m.   8:00 a.m.   8:30 a.m.

○ ● ○ ○ ○ ○ ● ○ ○ ○ ○ ○ ○

Step 4: From the number line, read the time Alex arrives at school.

Alex arrives at school at 8 a.m.

Answer the Question

Step 5: Alex will not be late for school. He will arrive on time.

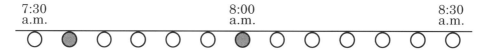 Now try these problems.

1. The tennis team decides to walk the $\frac{1}{2}$ mile from the town courts back to school. The walk takes them 8 minutes. They leave the town courts 15 minutes before band practice starts. How much time will they have at school before band practice?

Answer: They will have _____ minutes before band practice.

2. After work at the construction site, Greg walked to meet Manda at the hotel. Together they walked to the drugstore and then to the service station to pick up their car. From the construction site to the hotel is half a block. This distance is half the distance from the hotel to the drug store. The distance from the drugstore to the service station is twice the distance from the construction site to the drugstore. Circle the column that shows the number of blocks that Greg walks.

Construction site to hotel	$\frac{1}{2}$	$\frac{1}{2}$	$\frac{1}{2}$	$\frac{1}{4}$
Hotel to drugstore	1	$\frac{1}{4}$	1	$\frac{1}{2}$
Drugstore to service station	3	$1\frac{1}{2}$	2	$1\frac{1}{2}$

3. During the "Relay for Life," four members of the health club all walked about the same distance. Their four distances added to a total of 24 miles. What is the average distance they each walked?

A 4 miles **C** 6 miles

B 5 miles **D** 10 miles

4. When the ground is covered with snow, Logan often cross-country skis to work. The distance is only $\frac{1}{2}$ mile across a field. When there is no snow, Logan bikes to work. The distance is $1\frac{1}{2}$ miles on the road. It takes Logan about the same time to get to work by ski or by bicycle. If it takes her 10 minutes biking, how long does it take skiing?

Answer: It takes her _____ minutes.

☆ *Challenge Problem*
You may want to talk this one over with a partner.

Old Town is located on the banks and on two islands of a river. The town is connected by bridges. Is it possible to make a walking tour of the town and cross each bridge exactly once? If bridge X on the lower right side of the map collapses, could this still be done?

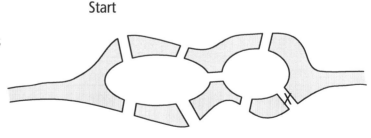

Start

♖ A Board Game (for Two or More Players)

The goal of this game is to move to each one of the 64 squares on the board. When you land on a square, you number it with the next counting number. Every move in this game is an L-shaped move—2 squares in one direction followed by 1 square at right angles. Then you label the square you land on with the next counting number.

Materials

Number cube to decide order of play.
Dry-erase *Maps & Directions* Board (on the next page), dry-erase marker, eraser, or a paper copy for each player.

Directions

1. Sit with players around the game board.

2. Each player tosses the number cube. The player with the highest number starts.

3. Player 1 makes any L-shaped move from the square labeled **1**. For example, the move might be two squares south and one square east to the square labeled **2**. From there player 1 continues to make L-shaped moves, labeling squares in order, 3, 4, 5, and so forth. When the player can only move to a square already numbered, this player's turn is over.

4. The next player starts over with a new board. Players take turns, always starting at square **1**.

5. The winner is the first player to label all the squares in increasing numerical order. If no one gets all the way through to 64, the player that gets closest wins.

✐ Before you play the game, try these warm-up problems.

1. The Kinships drive from the camp entrance to their campsite. They go 10 miles due east, 15 miles due south, 4 miles due west, and 2 miles due north. How many miles east and south of the park entrance is their campsite?

   A 6 miles east, 13 miles south   **C** 14 miles east, 13 miles south

   B 8 miles east, 11 miles south   **D** 14 miles east, 17 miles south

2. When Becky completes the *Maps and Directions* board, each row or column adds to 260. What is the average value for one square in row 8?

Game Board for *Maps & Directions*

1				**33**			
					19		
	2						
			45			**36**	
5							**60**
			26				
54							**11**

Lesson 5

→ *Traveling by Car*

Example Anderson has invited you to stay with his family for the summer. You have a car. You are going to drive the 1,500 miles to get to Anderson's house.

This chart shows the miles per gallon your car gets at different speeds. You travel at an average speed of 30 mph. Fill in the entries to complete the row for this speed.

Speed (miles per hour)	Miles per Gallon (mpg)	Total Number of Gallons	Total Cost of Gas at $1.75 per Gallon	Travel Time in Hours
30	20.5			
40	24.2			
55	24.0			
60	22.5			
70	19.2			

Solve

Step 1: Find the row that shows a speed of 30 mph. At this speed, the car goes 20.5 miles on one gallon of gas. Divide the total miles for the trip by the mpg for 30 miles per hour.

$1,500 \div 20.5 = 73.17$ The total gas used on the trip is 73.17 gallons.

Step 2: Find the total cost of gas by multiplying the number of gallons by the cost for each gallon.

$73.17 \times \$1.75 = \$128.05$ The total cost of gas is $128.05.

Step 3: Divide the total miles for the trip by the speed in miles per hour.

$1,500 \div 30 = 50$ The travel time is 50 hours.

Answer the Question

Step 4: The total cost of gas is $128.05. The travel time for the trip is 50 hours.

✐ **Now try these problems.**

Use the chart in the Example.

1. Nettie calculates the cost of gas and the travel time for the other speeds. Circle the row where she made a mistake.

40 mph	$108.47	37.5 hours
55 mph	$109.38	35 hours
60 mph	$116.67	25 hours
70 mph	$136.72	21.43 hours

2. You travel at a speed of 60 miles per hour for two hours. Then you travel at 40 miles per hour for one hour.
   a. How far will you travel in three hours?
   b. What is your average speed over the three-hour journey?

   Answer: a._____ **b.** _____

3. What are the advantages and disadvantages of driving at 40 mph instead of 70 mph? Circle the correct word to make each statement true.
   a. You will use <u>more/less</u> gas.
   b. The total cost of gas will be <u>higher/lower</u>.
   c. The trip will take <u>more/less</u> time.
   d. You may pay for <u>more/less</u> meals and lodging.

4. You decide to drive only 8 hours each day on the 1500-mile trip. You have budgeted $60 a day for a motel room. Gas costs $1.75 per gallon. What speed would you try to maintain if you want to minimize the cost of the trip?

   A 30 mph   **B** 40 mph   **C** 55 mph   **D** 70 mph

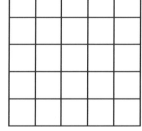

Starting→
Point

☆ *Challenge Problem*
You may want to talk this one over with a partner.

Here are the instructions for the road rally: Turn right at the first corner when coming from the east. Turn left at any corner other than the first corner when coming from another direction. The starting point for the rally is the most north-westerly corner of the rally grid. Mark the corners of a route that will bring a rally driver exactly back to the starting point. Are there any other routes? How far east can a rally route extend and why?

_____

_____

Review What You Learned

In this unit you have used mathematics to solve many problems. You have used mental math and estimation, practiced basic operations, solved equations, and used statistics.

These two pages give you a chance to review the mathematics you used and check your skills.

✔ Check Your Skills

1. The **A** bus makes a 2-hour round trip of town several times a day. It stops at the same places on every trip. Frank and Emily take a tour of the town by bus. They catch the bus at the bus stop outside their hotel. If they catch the 10 a.m. bus, when will they get back to their hotel?

    A 8 a.m.   **B** 10 a.m.   **C** 12 noon   **D** 2 p.m.

    If you need to review, return to lesson 1 (page 28).

2. On her bicycle, Jessica makes 4 pedal revolutions for every 7 wheel revolutions. How many pedal revolutions will she make for 350 wheel revolutions?

    Answer: _____

    If you need to review, return to lesson 2 (page 30).

3. James can pedal at about 40 pedal revolutions per minute. The circumference of the wheel tires on his bike is 87 inches. For every pedal revolution, the wheels make 1.75 revolutions.

    This expression finds D, the distance in inches that James travels in one minute. Complete the expression by filling the blank with the correct symbol: $+$, $-$, $\times$, or $\div$.

$$D = 40 \times 1.75 \_\_\_\_ 87$$

    If you need to review, return to lesson 2 (page 30).

4. Chris skateboards 2 miles to work when he misses the 5 p.m. bus. The trip takes him 20 minutes by skateboard. He needs to be at work by 5:45 p.m. What is the latest time he can leave home and still be on time for work?

Answer: _____

If you need to review, return to lesson 3 (page 32).

5. The Sheppards follow the walking tour guide of the city. From the hotel they go 10 blocks north, 8 blocks east, 5 blocks south, and 4 blocks west. Circle the point on the compass that tells where they will end up in relation to the hotel.

If you need to review, return to lesson 4 (page 34).

6. You plan to make a trip by car to a national park this summer. You estimate that the round trip is about 2,000 miles. You car gets 27 miles to the gallon at 55 mph. It gets 24 miles to the gallon at 70 mph.

   a. How many *less* gallons of gas will you have to buy if you average 55 mph instead of 70 mph?

   b. How much *less* time will you spend on the road if you average 70 mph?

Answer: a. _____ **b.** _____

If you need to review, return to lesson 5 (page 36).

Write Your Own Problem ✍

Choose a problem you liked from this unit. Write a similar problem using a situation and related facts from your own life. With a partner, share and solve these problems together. Discuss the mathematics and compare the steps you used. If you need to, rewrite or correct the problems. Write your edited problem and the answer here.

_____

_____

_____

_____

_____

_____

Unit 4

Managing Time

Preview

How You Will Use This Unit

Managing your time means deciding how best to use your time. You may need to figure out how long it takes to do something or to get somewhere. You may need to plan a schedule. You may want to phone or travel to a different time zone. As you work with time problems, you will often use math. The math skills you use include mental math and estimation, basic operations, equations, the vocabulary of geometry, and statistics.

What You Will Do in This Unit

In this unit, math steps demonstrate how to solve problems. These steps can help you answer questions such as these:

On average, you get two more hours of sleep a night on weekends than you get on the five weeknights. How many hours per night do you get on the weekends?

Your friend moves to the West Coast. You call her from the East Coast at 6 p.m. your time. What is the time for her when you call?

You are planning a summer music series that will take place each year. The series always begins on the first Friday in April, unless it is the first day of the month. The first Friday in April fell on April 4th in 2003. In which year will the first Friday next fall on April 1st?

You like to spend at least 10% of each day working on your favorite hobby. Yesterday you spent 1 hour of your 12-hour day on this hobby. Did you meet your goal?

What You Can Learn from This Unit

When you complete this unit, you will have used mathematics to work problems related to managing time. These problems are similar to those that may actually occur in your daily life.

Lesson 1

Sleep

Example Joe goes to bed at 10 p.m. every day. Every workday morning he sleeps until 6:30 a.m. On the first four days of his vacation, he sleeps until 7:30 a.m., 7:00 a.m., 8:00 a.m., and 8:30 a.m. What is the average amount of extra sleep he gets on a vacation day?

Solve

Step 1: Add the number of extra minutes Joe sleeps on his first four vacation days.

60 + 30 + 90 + 120 = 300   Joe sleeps a total of 300 extra minutes.

Step 2: To find the average, divide the number of hours by the number of mornings.

300 ÷ 4 = 75   His extra time averages 75 minutes (or 1 hour and 15 minutes) a day.

Answer the Question

Step 3: Joe sleeps an average of 1 hour and 15 minutes extra on vacation mornings.

✐ Now try these problems.

1. Peggy normally sleeps until 7:00 a.m. every school day. On the first four days of spring break, she sleeps until 9:30 a.m., 9:00 a.m., 7:30 a.m., and 8:00 a.m. What is the average amount of extra sleep she gets on spring break days? Circle the correct answer (in minutes).

60   90   120   150

2. Janetha gets an average of two more hours of sleep a night on weekends than she gets on weekdays. She gets about 7.5 hours of sleep a night on a weekday. Write one of these symbols: +, −, ×, or ÷, in the blank to make the statement true.

Janetha gets an average of (7.5 _____ 2) hours of sleep a night on weekends.

3. Ruben reads the following advice in a magazine article on insomnia. "If you can't fall asleep within 20 minutes of going to bed, get up and do something boring until you feel sleepy." On 4 nights out of 10, Ruben falls asleep right away. On the other nights he does not, so he gets up after 20 minutes. He does "something boring" for about 30 minutes each time. Over a 10-night period, about how many hours is he awake after first going to bed?

Answer: _____

4. About 56% of adult Americans in a survey report drowsiness sometime during the day. The survey reports responses from 3,600 adults. About how many of these adults report drowsiness?

A 1,620　　　**B** 2,016　　　**C** 3,600　　　**D** 6,428

5. Everyone needs a certain number of hours of sleep a night. When you get less hours than you need, you create a sleep debt. This sleep debt increases by the number of hours of sleep you lose each night. One way to reduce this sleep debt is to get extra sleep. Stewart has lost one hour of sleep a night for the last three nights. Put dots on the number line to show each of these three amounts. Label the dots with a, b, or c, and write an integer to name each dot.

a. Stewart's current sleep debt

b. Stewart's sleep debt after three more similar nights

c. Number of extra hours of sleep Stewart will need to make his sleep debt zero.

0

Answer: └──┴──┴──┴──┴──┴──┴──┴──┴──┴──┴──┴──┴──┘

☆ *Challenge Problem*
You need a partner for this one.

Ask your partner to choose any number. Then ask them to do the following operations: Multiply by 5. Add 4. Multiply by 2. Subtract 8. Divide by their original number. Tell them they should end up with the number 10. Work through the problem together to find out how you know the end number.

_____

You and your partner each then create a similar problem. Try your problem with your partner. Write your problem here.

_____

_____

Lesson 2

Example When Gayla and Minda were children, they lived about 50 miles apart in New York. They talked on the phone frequently. When Gayla graduated from high school she went to live in California. Minda usually calls Gayla at 9 p.m., New York time. What is the time for Gayla?

Solve

Step 1: On the time zone map, find California and New York. Write the time zone names for these two states, as shown on the map.

Pacific and **Eastern**

Step 2: Draw a number line and mark the location of the time zones.

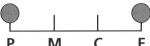

Step 3: The sun rises in the east, so it is 8 a.m. in New York before it is 8 a.m. in California. The time in the Pacific zone is 3 hours less than (or behind) the time in the Eastern zone. At 8 a.m. in New York, it is 5 a.m. in California.

Subtract 3 hours from Minda's time to find Gayla's time.

$9 - 3 = 6$ At 9 p.m. in New York, it is 6 p.m. in California.

Answer the Question

Step 4: When Minda calls Gayla at 9 p.m. Minda's time, it is 6 p.m. Gayla's time.

✏️ Now try these problems.

Use the time zone map in the Example.

1. James and Donovan used to live 5 minutes from each other. James got a new job and moved to Florida. Donovan stayed in central Texas to run the family farm. James usually calls Donovan at 10 p.m. James' time. What is the time for Donovan?

    A 7 p.m.   **B** 8 p.m.   **C** 9 p.m.   **D** 11 p.m.

2. Rachael won a scholarship to spend a year at a music school. She calls home to California. She says that her time is now 2 hours ahead of them. Shade the states on the map where Rachael could be.

3. Winston's family is doing a cross-country trip. So far they have crossed two time zones going west. How much time have they gained or lost since they started their trip?

    Answer: _____

4. Leaving Wyoming and traveling east, the Hicks stop in Ohio at 3 p.m. Wyoming time. How should they correct their watches? Draw in the hands on the watch face.

5. Ruben leaves home at 9 a.m. He drives east for 4 hours. He crosses into another time zone, and continues on. What is the local time when he stops for supper 6 hours later after he entered the new time zone?

    A 5 p.m.   **C** 7 p.m.

    B 6 p.m.   **D** 8 p.m.

⭐ *Challenge Problem*
You may want to talk this one over with a partner.

Place the integers 1, 2, 3, and 4 in the circles so that no two connected circles contain consecutive integers. How many different sequences can you write?

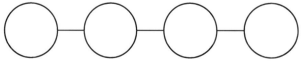

Lesson 3

The Small-Black-Circle Game

▲ A Game of Shapes (for Three to Six Players)

The goal of this game is to identify and name a shape as quickly as possible. First one player draws a shape. Then the rest of the players try to identify the shape by asking questions.

Materials

A *Small-Black-Circle Game* Chart, a number cube, and a stopwatch for timing.

Directions

1. Each player tosses the number cube. The player with the highest number starts. This is Player 1; the remaining players are Team 1.

2. Player 1 chooses one of the twenty-four shapes on the game chart without telling which one. Without letting the players on Team 1 see, Player 1 draws the chosen shape on paper. Then Player 1 starts the stopwatch.

3. The members of Team 1 take turns asking questions about the shape. The questions must be able to be answered with either Yes or No.

4. When Team 1 identifies the chosen shape, the time is up. Player 1 writes down the time it took Team 1 to correctly identify the shape. Player 2 then chooses shape and draws it. The remaining players form Team 2 and ask questions as they try to identify the shape.

5. The game continues with each player taking a turn. The winning team is the team that identifies the unknown shape in the least time.

✎ Before you play the game, try these warm-up problems.

1. Name each of the shapes on the game Chart using the language of math. For example, you might say "large gray pentagon" or "small white equilateral triangle."

2. The track is in the shape of a regular polygon. Todd runs completely around the track 3 times. He turns eight corners.

    What shape is the track, and where is the starting point? Explain your answer.

    Answer: _____

The *Small-Black-Circle* Game Chart

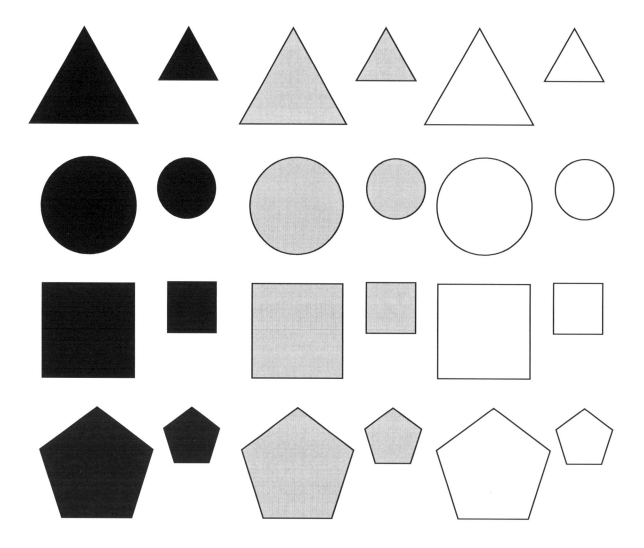

Example The music competition takes place in May for two consecutive days in one week. Then the finals are held during the next week on the same days of the week. Martin shades these four days on his calendar. These dates form a 2 × 2 block and the sum of the dates is 68. What four dates did Martin shade? Which date is the greatest in the shaded block?

MAY				28			29
Sun	**Mon**	**Tues**	**Wed**		**Thurs**		
					1		
4	5	6	7		8		
11	12	13	14		15		
18	19	20	21		22		
25	26	27					

Solve

Step 1: Use n for the greatest date in the block of dates. This is the last day of the finals. The value of n will be the answer to the last question. Use the language of math to write the date that is one less than n.

$n - 1$ This expression represents the next-to-last day of the finals.

Step 2: Use the language of math to write the dates that are a week earlier. Each date in the first week is 7 days earlier than the days of the finals.

$(n) - 7$ and $(n - 1) - 7$ These simplify to $n - 7$ and $n - 8$.

Step 3: Write an equation to show the sum of the dates for all four days of the contest.

$n + (n - 1) + (n - 7) + (n - 8) = 68$

Step 4: Solve this equation for n. Then find the other three dates by substitution.

$4n - 16 = 68$ Add the terms that contain n and add the integers.

$4n = 84$ Add 16 to each side of the equation.

$n = 21$ Divide each side by 4.

$n - 1 = 20$ $n - 7 = 14$ $n - 8 = 13$

Answer the Question

Step 6: Martin shaded May 13, 14, 20, and 21. The greatest date in the block is 21.

✏ Now try these problems.

Use the calendar in the example if needed.

1. *MayFest* is on the same two consecutive days of the week for two consecutive weeks in May. These dates form a 2 × 2 block and have a sum of 24. On the calendar, circle the 2 × 2 block of dates for *MayFest*.

2. Find a sequence of three dates in May where the middle number is the mean of the others. Exactly how many of these sequences are there?

    A 1   **B** 20   **C** 21   **D** 29

3. The first fund-raising meeting of the year is held on March 6, unless this is a Sunday. For dates from March 1 on, you can use the following rule. The date is always one day later in the week next year, unless next year is a leap year. If next year is a leap year, the given date will be two days later next year. March 6 falls on a Saturday in 2004. Remember that 2004 and 2008 are leap years. Circle the year(s) in which March 6 will fall on a Sunday.

   2005   2006   2007   2008   2009   2010   2011   2012   2013

4. The town's mayor serves three years, and the six council members each serve two years. The terms of three council members expire in the odd-numbered years. The terms of the other three expire in the even-numbered years. What is the greatest number of council members that the mayor will work with during the three-year term?

☆ *Challenge Problem*
You may want to talk this one over with a partner.

The World Future Society predicts future technology. The Society also predicts when these technologies will probably be in *common* use. Here are some of their predictions.

2006–2009: Neural networks, hybrid vehicles, computer sensory recognition

2012–2018: Distance learning, high-speed trains, intelligent transportation systems

2020–2030: Ceramic engines, gene therapy, artificial food, manned missions to Mars

In your opinion, which are *least* likely to happen on schedule, and why?

Example On her vacation, Nancy has a goal to spend at least 30% of each day on the beach. On the last day she spends 4 hours on the beach out of her 15-hour day. Did Nancy meet her goal on the last day?

Solve

Step 1: Calculate 30% of 15 hours.

$$30\% \text{ of } 15 = \frac{30}{100} \times 15$$
$$= 4.5$$

Her goal is 4.5 hours out of the 15.

Step 2: Compare the hours spent on her last day to the hours of her goal.

$$4 < 4.5$$ 4 is less than 4.5

Answer the Question

Step 3: Nancy did not meet her goal on the last day.

✏ Now try these problems.

1. Leah and Theo like to walk in the local shopping mall for 75% of their 1-hour lunch break. On Friday they started at 12 noon and walked for 45 minutes. Did they meet their daily goal? Shade the clock face to show what part of an hour 45 minutes is.

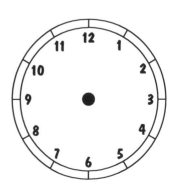

---

2. The table shows the number of hours Grant practices the flute each day.

Monday	Tuesday	Wednesday	Thursday	Friday	Saturday
2.5	1.5	1	3	1	3.5

  a. Monday's hours are what percent of the total number of hours?

  b. What is the mean number of hours he practices each day during this six-day period?

  Answer: a._____ **b.** _____

3. Luce earns $75 an hour. She pays the plumber $62 an hour, even though she knows how to fix the plumbing. How much more is her hourly pay than the plumbers?

  A $1.20   **B** $6.50   **C** $10   **D** $13

4. David visited the home improvements store 45 times in 1999 and 54 times in 2002. What is the percent of increase in the number of times that David visited the home improvements store from 1999 to 2002? To find percent of increase, divide the amount of change by the original amount. Write a math sentence to find the percent of increase.

  Answer: Percent of increase = (____ – ____) ÷ ____ × 100, OR

  Percent of increase = _____

5. Marcia spends 40% of her time at the amusement park on her favorite ride. She spends 30% on her second favorite ride, and 20% wandering around. The rest she spends in the snack bar. In total, she spends 6 hours at the amusement park. Circle the expression that gives the amount of time Marcia spends in the snack bar.

$$\frac{100 - (40 + 30 + 20)}{100} \times 6 \text{ hours} \qquad \frac{100 - (40 - 30 - 20)}{100} \times 6 \text{ hours} \qquad \frac{40 + 30 + 20}{100} \times 6 \text{ hours}$$

☆ *Challenge Problem*
You may want to talk this one over with a partner.

Cory starts working on his engine at about 10 a.m. and loses track of the time. The clock in the main hall strikes one time. On the hours, this clock strikes the number of the hour. For example, it strikes 3 times at 3:00. It strikes once at each half-hour. What is the maximum length of time he must wait to be sure what time it is? Explain.

_____

_____

Review

Review What You Learned

In this unit you have used mathematics to solve many problems. You have used mental math and estimation, practiced basic operations, solved equations, practiced geometry vocabulary, and used statistics.

These two pages give you a chance to review the mathematics you used and check your skills.

✔ Check Your Skills

1. Perry goes to bed at 10 p.m., and sleeps until 6:00 a.m. every workday morning. This week he sleeps until 7:30 a.m. on Saturday and on Sunday until 8:00 a.m. Perry goes to bed at the same time every day. What is the average time he gets up on a weekend morning? Draw the hands on the clock to show his average rising time for a weekend day.

   If you need to review, return to lesson 1 (page 41).

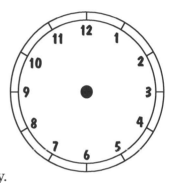

2. About 45% of adult Americans surveyed report having no problem staying awake the whole day. The survey shows responses from 2,000 adults. Use math language to show *n*, the number of adults who have no problem staying awake.

   Answer: *n* = _____ × _____

   If you need to review, return to lesson 1 (page 41).

3. Angelina and Henrietta lived next door to each other on the West Coast. Angelina got married and moved to Michigan. Michigan time is two hours different from West Coast time. When Henrietta calls Angelina, it is usually about 8 p.m. Henrietta's time. What is the time for Angelina?

   A 6 p.m.   **C** 9 p.m.

   B 7 p.m.   **D** 10 p.m.

   If you need to review, return to lesson 2 (page 43).

4. You are planning to start a summer music series that will continue for the next 5 years. This event is always on the first Friday in April, unless this is the 1st of the month. The first Friday in April fell on April 4th in 2003. Remember that 2004 and 2008 are Leap years. In which year will the first Friday next fall on April 1st?

Answer: _____

If you need to review, return to lesson 4 (page 47).

5. Christi is watching a series of documentaries that runs from 6 p.m. to 10 p.m. She gets a soda half way through the one-hour documentary that started at 7 p.m. What percent of the four-hour period has passed when she gets the soda? Shade the segment of the pie chart that shows this portion.

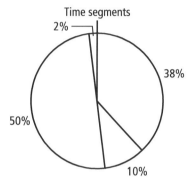

If you need to review, return to lesson 5 (page 49).

Write Your Own Problem ✍

Choose a problem you liked from this unit. Write a similar problem using a situation and related facts from your own life. With a partner, share and solve these problems together. Discuss the mathematics and compare the steps you used. If you need to, rewrite or correct the problems. Write your edited problem and the answer here.

_____

_____

_____

_____

Unit 5 — *Community*

Preview

How You Will Use This Unit

As part of a community, you can take advantage of many different things. You can use the post office and library and increase your education. You can apply for a passport for foreign travel, or get a license or permit to operate a vehicle or business. You can also take part in community activities. As you do these things, you will often use math. The math skills you use include mental math and estimation, basic operations, equations, and statistics.

What You Will Do in This Unit

In this unit, math steps demonstrate how to solve problems. These steps can help you answer questions such as these:

You sign up to take three courses. A week later you decide to withdraw from one course. How many credit hours are you now taking?

You take a stack of items to the post office to mail. Each item takes a different number of stamps. How can you quickly estimate the total cost of mailing all the items?

You borrow several books from the library for two weeks. You read the shortest book in two days. What is the mean number of days you have to read each of the other books?

A U.S. passport lasts ten years. You just applied for and received a new passport. How old will you be when it expires?

What You Can Learn from This Unit

When you complete this unit, you will have used mathematics to work problems related to being part of a community. These problems are similar to those that may actually occur in your daily life.

Example Jailyn signed up for 4 courses. Each course is worth 3 credit hours. Two weeks later she withdrew from one of the courses because of her work schedule. How many credit hours is she now carrying?

TUITION AND FEES

Credit Hours	Tuition	Athletic Fee	Computer Fee	Health Services	Library Use	Advisor Fee	Student Services	TOTAL
3	260	20	15	20	10	20	40	385
6	520	40	30	20	20	20	80	730
9	780	60	45	20	30	20	120	1,075
12	1,040	80	60	20	40	20	160	1,420
15	1,300	100	75	20	50	20	160	1,725
18	1,560	120	90	20	60	20	160	2,030
21	1,820	140	105	20	70	20	160	2,335

Solve

Step 1: Underline the words that tell the number of courses.

<u>4 courses</u>

Step 2: She withdrew from one course. Subtract 1 from the total number of courses.

$4 - 1 = 3$ She is now signed up for 3 courses.

Step 3: Underline the words that tell the credit hours per course.

<u>Each course is worth 3 credit hours.</u>

Step 4: Multiply her courses now by the number of credit hours per course.

$3 \times 3 = 9$ She is now signed up for 3 courses at 3 credit hours each.

Answer the Question

Step 5: Jailyn is now carrying 9 credit hours.

✎ Now try these problems.

Use the chart that shows Tuition and Fees.

1. Corbin signed up for 2 courses. Each course is worth 3 credit hours. One week later he added another course. How many credit hours is he now carrying?

2. Catherine wonders if she would pay less for each credit hour if she were to take more credit hours. She is currently signed up for 9 credit hours.

Use the Tuition and Fees chart. Calculate the cost per credit hour for 9 and for 12 credit hours. Then complete this statement:

The cost per credit hour for 12 credit hours is _____ the cost per credit hour for 9 credit hours.

    A equal to   **C** less than

    B more than   **D** $\frac{9}{12}$ times

3. Tobias needs 18 credit hours to graduate. He compares the cost of tuition at two colleges. At one college the tuition for 18 credit hours is $1,560. At the other college tuition is quoted at $88 per credit hour.

Circle the invoice from the college where tuition is *more* expensive.

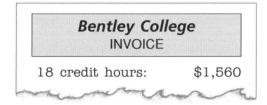

4. The restaurant where Bill works pays his tuition if he maintains a 3.0 grade point average. Bill signs up for 9 credit hours of courses.

    a. On the Tuition and Fees chart, circle each fee that Bill will still have to pay. What is the total amount that Bill will still have to pay?

    b. How much will Bill save if he maintains a 3.0 grade point average?

Answer: a. Bill will still have to pay $_____

        b. Bill will save $_____

☆ *Challenge Problem*
You may want to talk this one over with a partner.

Look at the Tuition and Fees chart. Why do you think the cost per credit hour decreases as the number of credit hours increases?

_____

_____

_____

Lesson 2

Example Gray takes a stack of letters, bills, and cards to the post office to mail. Twelve of his items each need a 37-cent stamp. Six items each need a 60-cent stamp. Two items each need an 83-cent stamp.

   a. What is a quick estimate of the total cost to mail these items?

   b. What is the mean cost per item based on this estimate?

Solve

Step 1: Make an organized chart of the items and stamp costs in the problem.

12 items	37 cents each
6	60
2	83

Use the language of math to write an expression for the total cost.

$(12 \times 37) + (6 \times 60) + (2 \times 83)$ cents

Step 2: Circle numbers for rounding to the nearest ten for easier estimation.

$(12 \times \boxed{37}) + (6 \times 60) + (2 \times \boxed{83})$

Round these numbers. Then multiply and add to estimate the total.

$(12 \times 40) + (6 \times 60) + (2 \times 80) = 480 + 360 + 160$

$\qquad\qquad\qquad\qquad\qquad = 1,000$ The total is 1,000 cents.

$\qquad\qquad\qquad\qquad\qquad = \$10.00$ Divide by 100 cents in 1 dollar.

Step 3: To find the mean cost per item, divide the total cost by the number of items.

$\$10.00 \div 20 = \$0.50$, or 50 cents

Answer the Question

Step 4: **a.** An estimate of the total cost of the stamps is $10.00.

   b. The mean cost per item based on this estimate is 50 cents. It cost Gray an average of about 50 cents to mail one of his items.

✏️ Now try these problems.

1. MaryRose takes a stack of items to the post office to mail. Eleven items need a 37-cent stamp each. Four items need a 25-cent stamp each. Five items need a $1.06 stamp each.

    a. What is an estimate of the total cost to mail these items?

    b. What is the mean cost per item based on this estimate?

    Answer: a._____ **b.** _____

2. Heather has a stack of letters to mail. She buys a sheet of 37-cent stamps for $7.40. One letter takes two stamps. The rest take one stamp each. How many letters can she mail?

    A 10   **B** 19   **C** 20   **D** 25

3. It costs Landon $6.35 to mail a package, and $3.13 to mail a large envelope. How much change should he get from $10? Show one way to make this change using the bills and coins shown. On the line below, write how many of each item you would use for his change.

_____   _____   _____   _____   _____

4. You can rent a small post office box for $24 a year. You can rent a large one for $66 a year. The charge for six months is half the annual rental charge plus $1. Use a to represent the rent for a year. Circle the math expression that gives the rent for six months.

    $\frac{a}{2} - 1$ $\frac{a}{2} + 1$ $a \times 2 - 1$ $a \times 2 + 1$

☆ Challenge Problem
You may want to talk this one over with a partner.

You are leaving early on Saturday, May 3 for 11 days of vacation. On May 1, you ask the post office to hold your mail starting Saturday. You return late on the eleventh day of your vacation. You are going to pick up the mail the day after you return. On what date and day of the week will you pick up your mail?

_____

_____

Example Linda borrows four science fiction books from the library for two weeks. She reads the shortest book in two days. She plans to finish all the books by the end of the two-week period. What is the mean number of days that Linda plans for reading each of the other books?

Solve

Step 1: Translate two weeks into days.

2 × 7 = 14   Each week has 7 days. There are 14 days in two weeks.

Step 2: Subtract the 2 days that Linda took to read the shortest book.

14 − 2 = 12   Linda has 12 days to read the 3 books she has left.

Step 3: Divide 12 by 3 to find the mean (or average) number of days for each book.

12 ÷ 3 = 4   Linda has 4 days to read each of the 3 books.

Answer the Question

Step 4: The mean number of days that Linda plans for reading each book is 4 days.

✏ Now try these problems.

1. Trey borrows six art books from the library for two weeks. After two days, he has finished the two shortest books. He wants to finish all the books by the end of the two-week period. What is the mean number of days Trey has to read each of the other books?

   Answer: _____

2. The library charges a fine of $0.25 per book per day for returning books late. SueAnn decides to create a chart that makes calculating fines quick and easy. Complete the chart that SueAnn has started.

	1 day	2 days	3 days	4 days	5 days	6 days	7 days
1 book	0.25	0.50	0.75	1.00	1.25	1.50	1.75
2 books							
3 books							
4 books							

3. Josh has a stack of overdue books. He pays his fine with one quarter, eight dimes, six nickels, and fifteen pennies. The fine per book per day os $0.25.

This picture shows 4 possible stacks of books that Josh might have. Under each stack, write how many days late the stack would be to match the fine.

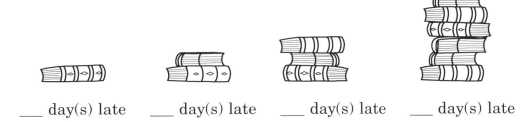

___ day(s) late   ___ day(s) late   ___ day(s) late   ___ day(s) late

4. You can use a library computer for an hour at a time. The cost is $1 an hour. The two library computers are used an average of 4 hours a day over a 6-day week. How much money will the library collect during the average week?

   A $6   **B** $8   **C** $24   **D** $48

☆ Challenge Problem
You may want to talk this one over with a partner.

On five days, the library took in $9.50, $17.75, $10.25, $18.00, and $11.25 in fines. What is the mean amount of money taken in per day? What do you need to know to find the average number of days late per book?

_____

_____

_____

_____

Lesson 4

A Passport to Travel

Example A United States of America passport is good for ten years. Crystal's passport was issued when she was 23 years old. How old will she be when it expires?

Solve

Step 1: Underline the statement that tells when Crystal's passport was issued.

<u>Crystal's passport was issued when she was 23 years old.</u>

Step 2: Add to this age the number of years that a passport lasts.

23 + 10 = 33   The passport expires ten years after it is issued.

Answer the Question

Step 3: Crystal will be 33 years old when her passport expires.

✐ Now try these problems.

1. Some foreign visas only last one year. Kalen's one-year foreign visa was issued when he was 19 years old. How old will he be when it expires?

   Answer: Kalen's foreign visa will expire when he is _____ years old.

2. A U.S. passport lasts ten years. The date of expiration on Marshall's U.S. passport is June, 2010. He was 15 years old when he got it. How old will he be when it expires?

   A 20 years old   **C** 30 years old

   B 25 years old   **D** There is not enough information.

3. John and Maggie need photos to renew their passports. Together they pay a total of $17.95 plus tax for two passport photos for each of them. The tax is 8%.

The following math expression gives the mean cost per photo, tax included. Fill in values for *x* and *y* to complete this math expression.

$$\frac{17.95\ (x)}{y}$$

4. The post office tells Katya that a passport will cost $55 and arrive in 6 weeks. However, she can pay $115 if she wants it in 2 weeks. Katya wants her passport in 3 weeks. What should she pay?

Circle the bills that make up this amount.

5. The post office tells Sheron that a passport will cost $55 and arrive in 6 weeks. However, he can pay more and get it sooner. Sheron needs his passport eight weeks from now. He wants to pay the lower fee. How long can he wait before applying for a passport?

Answer: Sheron can wait _____ weeks and _____ days.

☆ *Challenge Problem*
You may want to talk this one over with a partner.

Choose a three-digit number and write it down. Write the digits in reverse order to create a second number. Subtract the smaller number from the larger number. How many different results can you get when you subtract? What are the possible results? Write a math expression and an explanation to support your answers.

_____

_____

_____

♜ A Board Game (for Two or More Players)

The goal of this game is to acquire the most money. First you toss the number cube and move your counter around the board. Then you follow the directions on the square where you land.

Materials

Game board (on next page), counters or tokens of different colors, play money (100 $1,000 bills, 200 $100 bills, 100 each of $20 bills and $10 bills, 200 $5 bills), one number cube.

Directions

1. All players start with $2,500 and place their counter on **Start**. One player keeps the bank and collects and distributes money.

2. Each player in turn tosses the number cube. Then the player moves his or her counter that number of squares clockwise around the board. Follow the directions on the square the player lands on.

3. Fees, bills, and taxes are paid into the bank. Income is withdrawn from the bank.

4. When one player runs out of money, or has too little money to go on, the game stops. The winner is the player with the most money at the end.

✍ Before you play the game, try these warm-up problems.

1. Anthony needs a building permit that costs $100 so he can expand his house. He needs to renew his fishing/hunting license for $25. Taxes of $800 are due next week. How much money should he have available to pay these bills, with $100 left over?

   Answer: _____

2. Jill deposits her paycheck of $575 in the bank on Friday. On Saturday, she pays an electric bill of $90, a payment on her charge account of $300, and a parking fine of $20. How much does she have left out of her paycheck?

   Answer: _____

Government Services Board Game

Start	Pay $2 to visit city pool	Pay vehicle license of $30	Earn job bonus of $200	Pay water bill of $25
Pay $50 speeding ticket				Pay for dog permit $5
Pay fishing/ hunting license $85	City Park			Enjoy beach: take 2nd turn
Go vote: take 2nd turn				Buy building permit $100
Pay drivers license $35	City gets funding: take 2nd turn	EMS called for spider bite: go back 1 space	New job openings: pay $2 to apply	Pay dump fee $65

Review What You Learned

In this unit you have used mathematics to solve many problems. You have used mental math and estimation, practiced basic operations, solved equations, and used statistics.

These two pages give you a chance to review the mathematics you used and check your skills.

✔ Check Your Skills

1. Ben signed up for 5 courses. Each course is worth 3 credit hours. A week later he withdrew from one of the courses because of his work schedule. How many credit hours is he now signed up for?

Answer: _____

If you need to review, return to lesson 1 (page 54).

2. Lera compares the cost of tuition at two colleges. At Hill College, the tuition for 15 credit hours is $1,425. At Caldwell College, tuition is quoted per credit hour. Lera has figured out that the cost of tuition per credit hour is cheaper at Hill College. What could the cost of tuition per credit hour be at Caldwell College? Write in a number that satisfies Lera's conclusion.

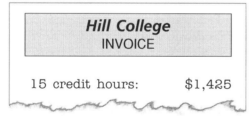

Hill College
INVOICE

15 credit hours: $1,425

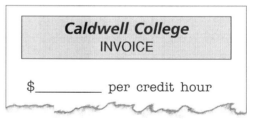

Caldwell College
INVOICE

$_____ per credit hour

If you need to review, return to lesson 1 (page 54).

3. You take a stack of letters, bills, and cards to the post office to mail. Seven items need a 37-cent stamp each. Four items need a 60-cent stamp each. Ten items need an 83-cent stamp each. What is a good estimate of the total cost to mail these items?

    A $6.03   **C** $24.40

    B $13.20   **D** $88.20

If you need to review, return to lesson 2 (page 56).

4. On Wednesday the thirteenth of the month, Craig borrows three library books for two weeks. He reads one book in three days. He calculates the mean number of days to read each of the other books. Based on this number, when should Craig start to read the third book so that he can finish all the books by the end of the two-week period? Circle that day.

Sun	Mon	Tues	Wed	Thurs	Fri	Sat
10	11	12	13	14	15	16
17	18	19	20	21	22	23
24	25	26	27	28	29	30

If you need to review, return to lesson 3 (page 58).

5. A U.S. passport lasts ten years. Kyla got her first passport three years ago, when she was 18 years old. How old will she be when it expires?

Answer: _____

If you need to review, return to lesson 4 (page 60).

Write Your Own Problem ✏️

Choose a problem you liked from this unit. Write a similar problem using a situation and related facts from your own life. With a partner, share and solve these problems together. Discuss the mathematics and compare the steps you used. If you need to, rewrite or correct the problems. Write your edited problem and the answer here.

_____

_____

_____

Preview

How You Will Use This Unit

Thinking about the future can involve many things. You may think about different career choices and the earnings that go with them. You may think about the cost of living and insurance. You may also think about how to make investments. As you compare options and make choices, you will often use math. The math skills you use include mental math and estimation, basic operations, equations, and statistics.

What You Will Do in This Unit

In this unit, math steps demonstrate how to solve problems. These steps can help you answer questions such as these:

You study a chart that shows information about various jobs. The chart shows typical low and high salaries for these jobs. What is the median salary for the job you are interested in?

You buy a second-hand car. You make monthly payments on it. You also have to pay for insurance and fuel. What is the average amount per month you will pay for your car?

You have $2,549 in your special investment account. You earn 7% interest on it. By how much does your account increase?

You study the income tax table for single people. You earn $25,800 taxable income this year. How much tax do you pay?

What You Can Learn from This Unit

When you complete this unit, you will have used mathematics to work problems related to your future. These problems are similar to those that may actually occur in your daily life.

(Lesson 1)

→ *Career Options*

Example Alberto looks at a survey that shows several jobs and their salaries. What is the range of the salaries for a ranch manager? What are the mean, median, and mode amounts of pay for beginning careers such as these? Use the amounts in the *Lowest Salary* column.

Career Options	Lowest Salary	Highest Salary
Farm Equipment Mechanic	$28,354	$43,140
Ranch Manager	$33,169	$40,114
Veterinarian	$57,227	$87,076
Customer Relations Manager	$40,913	$60,515
Banking and Commercial Loan Clerk	$29,787	$40,114

Solve

Step 1: Find the range of the salaries for ranch manager. Subtract the lowest salary from the highest salary.

$40,114 – $33,169 = $6,945   The range for this job is $6,945.

Step 2: Next, find the mean for all the amounts in the *Lowest Salary* column. To find the mean, find the sum of all the items. Then divide by the number of items.

$28,354 + $33,169 + $57,227 + $40,913 + $29,787 = $189,450
$189,450 ÷ 5 = $37,890   The mean lowest salary is $37,890.

Step 3: Arrange the amounts in the *Lowest Salary* column in order. The median is the middle data item, if there is one. Half of the salaries are above the median, and half are below the median. (If there are an even number of data items, the median is the average of the two items in the middle.)

$28,354 $29,787   ($33,169) $40,913 $57,227

Step 4: To find the mode of the lowest salaries, find the salary that occurs most often. No salary occurs more than once. There is no mode for these data items.

Answer the Question

Step 5: The range for the salaries for a ranch manager is $6,945. The mean and the median of the lowest salaries are $37,890 and $33,169. There is no mode.

✏️ Now try these problems.

1. Alberto shows Jake the survey (in example) of several jobs and their typical salaries. Jake wants to become a veterinarian. What is the range of the salaries for this job? What are the mean, median, and mode of the amounts in the *Highest Salary* column?

   Answer: The range of the salaries for a veterinarian is $_____.

   The mean, median, and mode of the salaries in the *Highest Salary* column are $_____, $_____, $_____.

2. Mary is a freelance writer. She earns money for each contract that she completes. The mean value of her earnings for the last three contracts is $2,150. Two of these three contracts were for $1,500 and $2,700. What was the value of the third contract?

   A $2,100   C $2,250

   B $2,116.67   D $2,700

3. Ray is an elementary school teacher. His total compensation is $66,700. What percent of his total compensation is each benefit? To match benefits with percents, draw a line from each amount to its percent.

Ray's Compensation Package

Base Salary	$46,690	5%
Social Security	$ 3,335	2%
401k	$ 2,668	9%
Disability	$ 1,334	3%
Healthcare	$ 6,003	7%
Pension	$ 2,001	4%
Time off	$ 4,669	70%

☆ *Challenge Problem*
You may want to talk this one over with a partner.

Louis and Craig each work 40 hours per week. Louis is paid $12 an hour. He is guaranteed a 5% annual increase. Craig is paid a salary of $400 a week. He is guaranteed a cost-of-living increase and a merit increase. Which package would you prefer and why?

_____

_____

_____

Lesson 2

Costs of Living

Example Brandon keeps a record of what he spends on food. Over the last six months, the mean amount he spent has been $85 a week. Then he was on vacation for a week and spent $127 on food. For the next three weeks he kept his spending the same each week. What did he spend each week to keep his mean at $85 over the seven-month period?

Solve

Step 1: Use *s* for the amount Brandon spends each of the last three weeks. The value of *s* will be the answer to the question. The mean for the last month is $85. So what he actually spent is the same as spending $85 for each of four weeks. Write a sentence in words to show how *s*, $127, and $85 are related.

$127 plus 3*s* is equal to 4 multiplied by $85.

Step 2: Now write the same sentence, using the language of math.

$127 + 3s = 4 \times 85$

Step 3: To solve this equation, first simplify. Then undo what has been done to *s*.

$3s = 340 - 127$
$s = 71$

Answer the Question

Step 4: He must spend $71 a week over the next three weeks to maintain a mean of $85.

✏️ Now try these problems.

1. Sue Ellen keeps a record of what she spends on entertainment. Over the last year, she spent a mean of $52 a month. This month

she only spent $16. What can she spend next month and still maintain a mean of $52?

Fill in the numbers to make the math sentence true. What amount can she spend next month?

Answer: 16 + _____ × s = _____ × _____   s = _____

2. This month, Jesse buys a second-hand truck. He pays $100 a month for it. He must also pay $150 a month for insurance. Fuel costs him about $40 a month. Next month, he will pay $522 to put a lift on the truck. He will have no other truck expenses for the next six months. What will be Jesse's mean cost per month for his truck over the next six-month period?

Answer: _____

3. For their seven-day vacation, Sam and Amanda budget $3 each for lunch per day more than they normally spend. They normally spend $6 each for lunch. How much do they anticipate spending together for lunch over their vacation?

    A $42   **C** $84

    B $63   **D** $126

4. Wallis discovers that she spends about 12.5% of her total weekly expenses on knickknacks for the apartment she shares. Her total weekly expenses are about $328. If she stops buying knickknacks (or incidentals), how much money will she save? Fill in the amount.

Rent: $115   Food: $90   Gas: $____   Entertainment: $____   Incidentals: $_____

☆ *Challenge Problem*
You may want to talk this one over with a partner.

On a business trip, Diane allows $23 a day for breakfast, lunch, dinner, and a snack. Use the numbers 1 through 9 (once each) to fill in the circles so that the sum along each side of the triangle equals 23. Each side shows three ways she can spend her money!

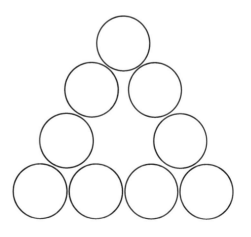

Lesson 3

Making Money

♠ A Card Game (for Two or More Players)

The goal of this game is to increase the value of your investment. First, you toss the number cube. Then you draw a card and follow directions.

Materials

Deck of event cards (on the next page), tally sheet, one number cube.

Directions

1. Title each column on the tally sheet with the name of one player. Write $1,000 under each name. This is the amount of money that each player starts with in a special investment account.

2. Player 1 tosses the number cube, picks the next card off the deck, and follows the directions: Replace x on the card with the number showing on the number cube. Make the calculation on the amount in your special investment account, as directed by the card. Write this new value in as the next entry under your name on the tally sheet. This is the new amount in your special investment account.

3. Players take turns tossing the number cube, picking the next card off the deck, and following the directions. The other players check the calculations.

4. The game ends when one player's special investment account goes to zero or below.

5. The winner is the player with the most money in the special investment account.

✎ Before you play the game, try these warm-up problems.

1. Maria has $3,250 in her special investment account. She earns 6% interest on it. Circle the correct amount of interest.

$195 $1,950 $3,445

2. Paul wants to find a high-risk, high-return investment. He wants to invest $$D$ and end up with $$D^2$. He plans to invest $1,000. How much does he expect to have at the end of his venture?

Answer: _____

Making Money Event Cards

A windfall: Add x to your investment account.	**Pay unexpected expenses:** Subtract $$x$ from your investment account.	**Company has a great new product:** Multiply investment account by x.
Lucky investment: Increase investment account by $10 to the power of x.	**Unlucky investment:** Divide investment account by 10.	**Earned interest:** Add $x\%$ to investment account.
Earned interest: Add $$x^2$ to your investment account.	**A windfall:** Add $$10x$ to your investment account.	**Company fails:** Reduce investment account to $100.
Pay taxes: Subtract $x\%$ from your investment account.	**Increase your investment:** Add $$100x$ to your investment account.	**Company has legal problems:** Subtract $$10x^2$ from investment account.
Share your investments: Give $9x\%$ to family members.	**A small windfall:** Multiply investment account by $\sqrt{x}$.	**A small loss:** Divide investment account by $\sqrt{x}$.
Contribute to charity: Subtract x^2 from investment account.	**Risky investment:** Divide investment account by x^2.	**Pay expenses:** Subtract $\frac{1}{x}$ of investment account.

Example Greg studies the income tax rate table for single people. He earns a salary of $36,500 a year as a ranch manager. How much tax does he owe?

Single Income Tax Rate Table

Taxable Income	Tax
Up to $27,050	15% of every dollar
$27,051 to $65,550	$4,057.50 plus 27.5% of the amount over $27,050
$65,551 to $136,750	$14,645.00 plus 30.5% of the amount over $65,550
$136,751 to $297,350	$36,361.00 plus 35.5% of the amount over $136,750
Over $297,350	$93,374.00 plus 39.1% of the amount over $297,350

Solve

Step 1: Underline the chart line that fits Greg's income.

$27,051 to $65,550 $4,057.50 plus 27.5% of the amount over $27,050

Step 2: To find the amount over $27,050, subtract $27,050 from Greg's salary.

$36,500 − $27,050 = $9,450

Step 3: Multiply to find 27.5% of $9,450.

$$27.5\% \text{ of } \$9,450 = \left(\frac{27.5}{100}\right) \times \$9,450$$
$$= \$2,598.75$$

Step 4: Add this percent to the base tax from the chart of $4,057.50.

$2,598.75 + $4,057.50 = $6,656.25

Answer the Question

Step 5: Greg owes $6,656.25 in income tax.

✏ Now try these problems.

1. As a customer relations manager, Martha makes $42,000 a year. Use the chart to calculate how much tax she owes.

   Answer: Martha owes _____ in tax.

2. In the year 2000, the government sent out over 91 million tax-refund checks. The average size of a tax-refund check was $1,650. These people paid too much tax, so they got a refund. Suppose this money had instead been in a savings account at 5% per year.

How much would the tax payer have earned on this amount? What might a tax payer buy with this interest, if too much tax had NOT been paid? Circle one of these items to show what this amount of lost interest could buy.

3. Andrew has started a website consulting business. He will pay taxes quarterly. To find out how much he should pay, he uses last year's tax information. Last year he paid $6,500 in taxes. From this he deducts $2,300 for tax already withheld from his income. He divides the result by 4 for each quarterly payment. He thinks he should pay $1,500 each quarter. Is he correct? If not, correct his calculations to show the right amount.

1040-ES Department of the Treasury Internal Revenue Service	**2005** Payment Voucher **1**	
File only if you are making a payment of estimated tax by check or money order. Mail this voucher with your check or money order payable to the "**United States Treasury**." Write your social security number and "2005 Form 1040-ES" on your check or money order. Do not send cash. Enclose, but do not staple or attach, your payment with this voucher.	**Calendar year–Due April 15, 2004**	
	Amount of estimated tax you are paying by check or money order	Dollars *1,500* | Cents *00*
Your first name and initial	Your last name	Your social security number

4. You are thinking about buying a home. It is valued at $70,000 in the assessment for taxes. The local school board has set a property tax rate of 1.59%. How much will you pay in property taxes to the school district in a year?

     A $70   **B** $111.30   **C** $700   **D** $1,113

☆ Challenge Problem
You may want to talk this one over with a partner.

Janice owes $7,524 in taxes. She asks her tax accountant what would happen if she does not pay her taxes this year. She learns that next year she would have to pay penalties and interest of about 10% on $7,524. How much interest would her investment have to earn to make this pay? How much would she have to pay in total taxes next year? Could she invest that amount and earn more interest than the penalties and interest she would owe? Would you do this? Explain.

Example Daniel pays $195 monthly for his health insurance package. The amount of his deductible is $1,000. This means he pays the first $1000 of medical bills before his insurance starts to pay. Joey pays $140 monthly for his health insurance package. The amount of his deductible is $2,000.

At the end of the year, both Daniel and Joey have medical bills of $1,800. Who spends more money in this year for health expenses? By how much?

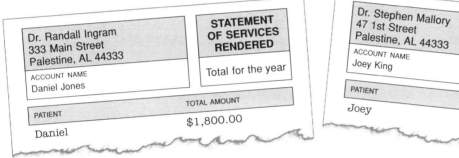

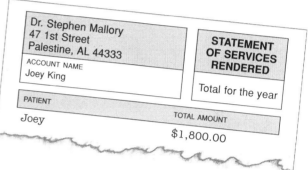

Solve

Step 1: Calculate how much Daniel pays per year for his insurance package.

$195 × 12 = $2,340

Step 2: Daniel's medical expenses are more than his deductible. This means that he pays only his deductible. Add the deductible to his monthly payments.

$2,340 + $1,000 = $3,340

Step 3: Joey's deductible is more than his medical expenses. So Joey must pay all of his medical expenses.

$140 × 12 = $1,680   This is the total of Joey's monthly payments.

$1,680 + $1,800 = $3,480   This is his expenses for the year.

Answer the Question

Step 4: Joey will pay $140 more than Daniel.

✏ Now try these problems.

1. Judith pays $205 a month for her health insurance package. Her deductible is $1,000. Mindy pays $149 a month for her health

insurance package. Her deductible is $2,500. At the end of the year, both Judith and Mindy's medical expenses are $1,500. Who pays more money? By how much?

Answer: _____ pays $_____ more than _____ .

2. Alex buys a second-hand truck. He must pay $1,800 a year for insurance. He plans to pay the insurance in twelve equal monthly installments. How much will he pay each month? Circle the correct amount.

$15 $24 $150 $200 $300 $450 $600

3. As part of her automobile insurance package, Shelbi pays $12 a year for towing. The insurance company will only pay $75 for each tow. Shelbi's car breaks down outside town. The towing company charges her $95 to tow it back into town. How much will the insurance company pay, and how much must Shelbi pay? Fill in Shelbi's calculation on the calculator screen.

95 – _____ = _____

4. Denny buys flight insurance at the airport on his way to a job interview. He pays $29.99 for $1,000,000 insurance. How much will his beneficiaries receive if the plane goes down and he loses his life?

A $29.99

C $1,000,000

B $999,970.01

D nothing

☆ Challenge Problem
You may want to talk this one over with a partner.

J. L. takes out insurance when he signs on to play football with a football team. The team also takes out insurance on J. L. What are possible reasons why J. L. and the team do this?

_____

_____

_____

_____

_____

Review What You Learned

In this unit you have used mathematics to solve many problems. You have used mental math and estimation, practiced basic operations, solved equations, and used statistics.

These two pages give you a chance to review the mathematics you used and check your skills.

✔ Check Your Skills

1. Kathy looks at data on the two jobs she is interested in. What is the difference in the mean salary for these two jobs?

Career Options	Lowest Salary	Highest Salary
Elementary School Teacher	$37,295	$58,771
Parks & Recreation Administrator	$28,120	$40,114

Answer: _____

If you need to review, return to lesson 1 (page 67).

2. This month, Marni buys a second-hand jeep. She pays $95 a month for it. She must also pay $145 a month for insurance. Fuel costs her about $50 a month. Next month, she will pay $723 to install a new stereo system. These are all the costs she will have for a while for her jeep. Complete Marni's calculation to find her average monthly costs over the next six months for her jeep.

$ ___ ÷ 6 = $ ___

If you need to review, return to lesson 2 (page 69).

3. Mark has $4,530 in his special investment account. He earns 5.5% interest on it. By how much does his account increase? Circle the correct answer.

$24.92 $249.15 $453 $823.64 $2,491.50

If you need to review, return to lesson 3 (page 71).

4. Lee looks at the income tax rate table for single people. As a car mechanic, he earns $32,900 a year. How much tax does he pay?

Single Income Tax Rate Table	
Taxable Income	**Tax**
Up to $27,050	15% of every dollar
$27,051 to $65,550	$4,057.50 plus 27.5% of the amount over $27,050
$65,551 to $136,750	$14,645.00 plus 30.5% of the amount over $65,550

A $566.00 **C** $5,666.25

B $4,935 **D** $9,047.50

If you need to review, return to lesson 4 (page 73).

5. Ellen pays $175 a month for her health insurance package. Her deductible is $1,000. At the end of the year, her medical bills are $2,367. How much of her medical bills does Ellen not have to pay?

Answer: _____

If you need to review, return to lesson 5 (page 75).

Write Your Own Problem ✐

Choose a problem you liked from this unit. Write a similar problem using a situation and related facts from your own life. With a partner, share and solve these problems together. Discuss the mathematics and compare the steps you used. If you need to, rewrite or correct the problems. Write your edited problem and the answer here.

_____

_____

_____

_____

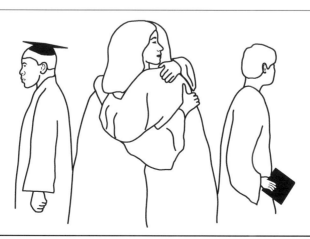

Unit 7

Thrifty Thinking

Preview

How You Will Use This Unit

Thrifty thinking means thinking about what you need and what you do. When you are a thrifty thinker, you get the most for your money. You can make choices in ways that are cost effective. Sometimes it is more cost effective to do things yourself. Sometimes it is more cost effective to look for sales and bargains. As you consider your choices, you will often use math. The math skills you use include mental math and estimation, basic operations, equations, and statistics.

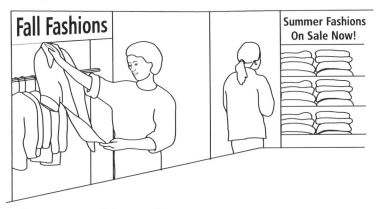

What You Will Do in This Unit

In this unit, math steps demonstrate how to solve problems. These steps can help you answer questions such as these:

You buy two shirts marked the same and get the second at half price. The first shirt costs $20. How much do you spend and how much do you save?

You like to go out to lunch once a week with friends. You usually spend about $6. On the other days you take your lunch. What is the average, or mean, amount you spend on lunch?

You buy all the food for a camping trip at the local discount supermarket. Normally you pay $2.69 for a box of cereal. Here you pay $15 for ten times that amount. How much do you save?

You carpool to school with a friend to save gas. The round trip is 75 miles. Both your car and your friend's get 25 miles to the gallon. Gas costs $1.39 a gallon. How much do you save per trip by sharing the ride?

What You Can Learn from This Unit

When you complete this unit, you will have used mathematics to work problems related to thinking in thrifty ways. These problems are similar to those that may actually occur in your daily life.

Lesson 1

→ *Sales & Bargains—Shop 'Til You Drop!*

♜ A Board Game (for Two or More Players)

The goal of this game is to see who spends the most and who saves the most money. First, you throw the number cube. Then you move your counter and follow the directions.

Materials

Game board (on the next page), money cards (10 cards each for $10, $15, $20, $30, $60), clock with moveable hands, counters in a different color for each player, tally sheet (to keep a record of what everyone spends and saves), one number cube.

Directions

1. Choose a counter color for each player. Sit with players around the game board. Set the clock to 11:30 a.m.—the time that you all arrive at the shopping mall. Shuffle the money cards and place them face down on the board.

2. Everyone starts from the Food Court. You can move clockwise or counterclockwise. Continue to move in this direction for the rest of the game.

3. Player 1 tosses the cube and moves counter a matching number of squares. Read the directions for the square where the counter lands. Pick up a money card from the stack to find the value of any item purchased. (Replace the card on the bottom of the money card stack.) Follow the directions to find how much you have spent and saved. Record these values on the tally sheet.

4. Players take turns tossing the number cube, moving their counters, following directions, and recording how much they have spent and saved. Every time Player 1 takes a turn, the clock ticks forward 15 minutes. Remember to advance the clock!

5. The game is over when the mall closes at 11 p.m. The winner is the player who has spent the least and saved the most!

✏ Before you play the game, try this warm-up problem.

1. Adam buys two shirts each marked $20 and gets the second at half price. How much does he spend and save?

   A He spends $30 and saves $10.   **C** He spends $40 and saves $10.

   B He spends $20 and saves $20.   **D** He spends $40 and saves $20.

Game Board for *Shop 'Til You Drop!*

Felicia's Art Gallery & Gift Shop: 20% off anything before 2 p.m.	**Fishing & Hunting Emporium:** Buy a $45 rod, and get 10% off reel.	**Everyone's T-shirts:** Get 2 tops for the price of 1.	**WinBig Games Arcade:** Play the game machines (miss 1 turn). Lose $4.25	**BabiesAreNow Gift Shop:** Buy outfit for friend's new baby. Get $5 toy at $\frac{1}{2}$ price.
Run into a friend and stop to chat (miss 1 turn).		**Rest-A-While Food Court:** Stop and relax (miss 1 turn). Get an ice cream for $1.25. Start back where you left off. For **first** move, choose any square as start.		**ABC Fitness:** Try fitness machine (miss 1 turn). Get $10 certificate to club.
EveryDay Things: Buy 2 pairs of blue jeans. Get $15 T-shirt free.				**Coffee's Up:** Get cappuccino for $2.60 (miss 1 turn).
Greetings-To-All: Buy greeting cards and wrapping paper. Get 5% off total.		**MONEY CARDS**		**The Shoe Place:** Buy one pair of sneakers. Get second pair at $\frac{1}{2}$ price before 1 p.m.
Kitchens, Etc: 10% off everything before 3 p.m.	**ToYourHealth Vitamin Store:** Buy 2 identical bottles. Get $5 off second one.	**Time to Rest:** You need to regroup. Go to the Food Court.	**BookMark Book Store** Buy 1 book at $\frac{1}{2}$ price.	**All Things Iced:** Buy ice chest at 10% off.

Example Tessa likes to go out to lunch once a week with friends. She usually spends about $6. On the other days she makes her lunch. It takes her 15 minutes to make her lunch. The cost of the lunch she makes is only $2.50 a day. How much money does she save on a day when she makes her lunch? Over a 5-day week, how much time does she spend making her lunch? Over a 5-day week, what is the mean amount of money she spends per day on lunch?

Solve

Step 1: Subtract the cost of her homemade lunch from the amount she spends when she goes out.

$6 – $2.50 = $3.50

Step 2: Multiply the number of days she makes her lunch by the time she spends each day.

4 × 15 minutes = 60 minutes or 1 hour

Step 3: To find the mean cost, find the total for the week. Then divide by 5.

4 × 2.50 + 6 = 16
16 ÷ 5 = $3.20

Answer the Question

Step 4: Tessa saves $3.50 on a day when she makes her lunch. Over a 5-day week, she spends 1 hour making her lunch. Over a 5-day week, she spends a mean of $3.20 per day on lunch.

✎ Now try these problems.

1. Josh and his three friends split a pizza on Monday evenings. They spend about $3.30 each. On other evenings Josh makes a snack. It takes him 5 minutes to make for a cost of $1.50. How much money does he save on a day when he makes a snack? Over the 5-day week, how much time does he spend preparing his snack?

Over the 5-day week, what is the mean amount of money he spends per evening on a snack?

Answer: He saves _____. He takes _____.

He spends a mean of _____ per evening.

2. Jocelyn finds that the best price to buy a cover for her grandmother's sofa is $250. She goes to a fabric store and buys fabric for $96. She buys supplies for $12.50. She spends 10 hours making the cover. Her grandmother pays her $7 an hour. Fill in the details of the costs. What is the total cost for the cover? How much money does Jocelyn save?

Fabric:	$96.00
Supplies:	$_____
Labor:	$_____
TOTAL cost:	$_____

Answer: _____

3. Craig and Alyn rebuild a boat engine. The cost of parts is $300. It takes them 5 days, working 6 hours each day. They take time off from their regular jobs to do it. In their regular jobs, they earn about $9 an hour each. They know the local marine shop would have charged them $850 to do the job. Was it worth it to do the job themselves? Why?

Answer: _____

☆ Challenge Problem
You may want to talk this one over with a partner.

The youth club is selling hot dogs for a community event. Tom's FoodMarket donates the hot dogs. Three young people have food handler's licenses. They sell the hot dogs for $1.50 each. What things might you think about as you figure the cost of the event?

_____

_____

_____

_____

Example Sarah and George buy all the food for the camping trip at the local discount supermarket. Usually they pay $2.69 for a 16-ounce box of cereal. Here they pay $15 for ten times that amount. What does 16 ounces of the discount cereal cost? How much do they save on every 16 ounces of cereal by buying in bulk?

Solve

Step 1: Write a sentence in words that describes their $15 purchase.

They buy 10 times 16 ounces of cereal for a cost of $15.

Step 2: Use c for the *cost* of 16 ounces of discount cereal. Now write the sentence using c and the language of math.

$10 \times c = 15$

Step 3: Solve for c.

$c = 1.50$

Step 4: To find how much they save per 16 ounces of cereal, subtract the discount price from the normal price.

$$\$2.69 - \$1.50 = \$1.19$$

Answer the Question

Step 5: Each 16 ounces of discount cereal costs $1.50. They save $1.19 on every 16 ounces of cereal.

✏ Now try these problems.

1. Sarah and George buy bread for the camping trip at the local discount supermarket. Usually they pay $1.79 for a loaf. Here they pay $11 for twenty of the same loaves. What does one loaf of

the discount bread cost? Write in this number on the price tag. How much do they save per loaf by buying in bulk?

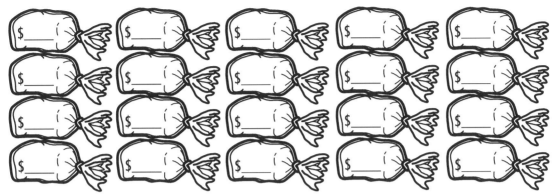

Answer: Sarah and George save $_____ per loaf.

2. The ice company charges $0.50 for one bag of ice. The company gives a 5% discount for 50 bags, a 10% discount for 100 bags, and a 25% discount for 250 bags. The marina buys 250 bags of ice. What total amount do they pay?

   A $93.75   **B** $112.50   **C** $118.75   **D** $125

3. Maria buys 1,000 makeup packs for $4.50 each. She sells them in blocks of 100 to friends for $7 each. Her friends then sell them to individual customers for $8 each. Circle one amount in each column that shows Maria's present expenses, income, and profit for these makeup packs.

Expenses	Income	Profit
1,000 × $4.50	100 × $8	100 × $2
100 × $7	1 × $4.50	1,000 × $2.50
1 × $8	1,000 × $7	1 × $8

☆ *Challenge Problem*
You may want to talk this one over with a partner.

You are moving to your own apartment. You need boxes to pack your stuff. The local moving company advertises "Box Truckload Sale." The company buys in volume and says that they pass the savings on to you. The office supply company sells boxes. The local supermarket gives away used boxes, but you have to get them on a certain day. Where would you go for boxes and why?

_____

_____

Lesson 4

New versus Used

Example Kirsten pays $4,500 for a second-hand car. Three years later she sells it for $3,900. Tanya pays $13,900 for a new car. Three years later she sells it for $5,500. How much are the cars costing Kirsten and Tanya per year? What are some possible reasons for the difference?

Solve

Step 1: Find the difference between what Kirsten pays for her car and her selling price. Subtract $3,900 from $4,500. Then, because she kept the car for 3 years, divide by 3. The result is the cost per year.

$4,500 − $3,900 = $600

$600 ÷ 3 = $200

Step 2: Do the same for Tanya. Subtract $5,500 from $13,900. Then divide by 3.

$13,900 − $5,500 = $8,400

$8,400 ÷ 3 = $2,800

Answer the Questions

Step 4: Kirsten's car cost her $200 per year. Tanya's car cost her $2,800 per year. The value of a new car goes down quickly in the first few years. A newer car will nearly always cost more per year than an older car. However, older cars may need more repairs.

✏ Now try these problems.

1. Paula buys a new wardrobe for the fall. It cost her $315.69. Maggie goes to garage sales and resale shops. She buys her new fall wardrobe for $15.00. The fall season has about three months. How much do these two wardrobes cost them per month over the fall season? What are some possible reasons for the difference?

   Answer: Paula's wardrobe costs her $_____ per month.

   Maggie's wardrobe costs her $_____ per month.

2. The Alexanders refill water bottles from the fresh water machines outside the supermarket. They spend $0.30 for each 1-gallon bottle. The Barnetts buy new water bottles. They spend $0.89 per 1-gallon bottle. Each family buys about 14 gallons of water in one month. How much more do the Barnetts spend for water? Circle the correct expression.

14 × ($0.89 − $0.30)

14 × $0.89 − $0.30

$0.89 − $0.30

$0.89 × 14

Sparkling Spring Water

3. Greg likes to listen to CDs. Over the summer, he buys 15 new ones for an average price of $17 each. He also buys 10 old ones for an average of $8.50 each. He borrows 7 from the library and friends at no cost. What are the mean and the mode of the cost per CD to Greg for these 32 CDs?

A mean: $10.63; mode: $8.50   **C** mean: $12.75; mode: $17

B mean: $13.60; mode: $8.50   **D** mean: $10.63; mode: $17

4. Diane wants to frame a new picture. She finds an old picture frame in her attic, but she doesn't like it. She takes the old frame to an antique dealer who gives her $100 for it. Then she pays $25 for a more modern picture frame at the local frame shop. How much money has she made?

Answer: _____

☆ *Challenge Problem*
You may want to talk this one over with a partner.

James pays $760 for a new air conditioning unit. It lasts him 5 years. Tony pays $200 for a used unit. It lasts him 2 years. In your opinion, which is the better deal, and why?

_____

_____

_____

Example Christine and Peg carpool to school to save gas. The round trip is 75 miles. Both Christine's and Peg's cars get 25 miles to the gallon. Gas costs about $1.39 a gallon. How much do they save together per round trip by sharing the ride in a car pool?

Solve

Step 1: First, write a sentence in words. Relate the gallons of gas used to the miles for one round trip.

75 miles divided by 25 miles per gallon gives the gallons of gas for one round trip.

Step 2: Now write the same sentence, using the language of math.

$\frac{75}{25} = 3$

Then multiply the gallons for a trip by the cost of each gallon of gas.

3 × $1.39 = $4.17   This product is the cost of one round trip.

Step 3: How many car trips do they save by car pooling? Draw a diagram to show the number of round trips if they each drive. Cross out one to show that both ride together when they carpool.

They make one trip together instead of one trip each. This means that they save the cost of one round trip each day.

Answer the Question

Step 4: Together they save about $4.17 per trip.

✏ Now try these problems.

1. Gwen, Will, and Randy car pool to school to save gas. The round trip is 52 miles. Their cars each get about 26 miles to the gallon. Gas costs about $1.65 a gallon. How much do they save together per trip by car pooling?

   Answer: Together they save about $_____ per trip.

2. Tim turns off the heat in his apartment when he goes to work. He turns it back on to 72° when he comes home. His monthly bill is $268. Lewis leaves the heat on all day, every day, at 68°. His monthly bill is $265. Why do you think the bills are almost equal?

   _____

   _____

3. Craig makes telephone calls whenever he thinks about it. Long-distance calls cost 5 cents a minute on the weekend and 7 cents a minute on weekdays. Last month he made 92 minutes of long-distance calls on weekends. He made 185 minutes of long-distance calls on weekdays. Complete Craig's telephone bill.

Starr Telephone Company
STATEMENT

Weekend long-distance calls	$_____
Weekday long-distance calls	$_____
If you made all your long-distance calls on the weekend, you would have saved	$_____

☆ Challenge Problem
You may want to talk this one over with a partner.

Gary leaves his car on one side of the ferry when he comes to work. The ferry ride is free. He unhooks his bike from the back of his car, walks onto the ferry with it, and bikes to work when he gets to the other side. What do you think are the advantages and disadvantages of doing this? What does it cost him? What does he save?

_____

_____

_____

Review What You Learned

In this unit you have used mathematics to solve many problems. You have used mental math and estimation, practiced basic operations, and solved equations.

These two pages give you a chance to review the mathematics you used and check your skills.

✔ Check Your Skills

1. You buy two shirts with the same price tag. You get the second at half price. The first shirt costs $15. How much do you spend and save? Complete the sales invoice and answer the question.

Sales Invoice	
Item	**Price**
First shirt:	$15
Second shirt at half price:	$_____
TOTAL (without tax):	$_____

   Answer: You spend $_____ and you save $_____.
   If you need to review, return to lesson 1 (page 80).

2. Jon-Michael goes out to lunch once a week with friends. He usually spends about $7. On the other days he makes his lunch. The lunch he makes only costs him $2.00 a day. How much money does he save on a day when he makes lunch? Over a 5-day week, what is the mean amount of money he spends per day on lunch?

   A $2; $1.80   **C** $5; $3

   B $5; $1.80   **D** $2; $3

   If you need to review, return to lesson 2 (page 82).

3. Harry and Jay rebuild a car engine. The cost of parts is $275. It takes them 4 days, working 5 hours each day. They take time off from their regular jobs to do it. In their regular jobs, they earn about $8 an hour each. Circle the expression that tells the number of dollars this project costs them.

   $275 + 2 \times 4 \times 5 \times 8$ $2 \times (275 + 4 \times 5 \times 8)$ $(275 + 4 \times 5) \times 8$

   If you need to review, return to lesson 2 (page 82).

4. Katy and CorieMae buy all the items for a camping trip at the local discount market. Usually they pay $2.50 for a pack of paper plates. Here they pay $12 for ten times that amount. Complete the equation that tells how much they save per pack by buying in bulk?

$2.50 − ($_____ ÷ _____) = $_____

If you need to review, return to lesson 3 (page 84).

5. Emily decides to take two classes on Monday nights instead of one on Mondays and one on Wednesdays. The round trip to the building where classes are held is 42 miles. Her car gets 28 miles to the gallon. Gas costs about $1.58 a gallon. How much does she save per week by making only one trip instead of two?

Answer: _____

If you need to review, return to lesson 5 (page 88).

Write Your Own Problem ✎

Choose a problem you liked from this unit. Write a similar problem using a situation and related facts from your own life. With a partner, share and solve these problems together. Discuss the mathematics and compare the steps you used. If you need to, rewrite or correct the problems. Write your edited problem and the answer here.

_____

_____

_____

_____

_____

_____

_____

_____

_____

Sustaining the World

Preview

How You Will Use This Unit

Sustaining the world is all about being responsible with our natural resources and the environment. It can mean protecting the environment for wildlife, endangered species, and ourselves. It can mean recovering resources to use again by recycling. It can mean managing waste more effectively. As you consider options, you will often use math. The math skills you use include mental math and estimation, basic operations, equations, and statistics.

What You Will Do in This Unit

In this unit, math steps demonstrate how to solve problems. These steps can help you answer questions such as these:

The recycle center charges different fees for depositing different types of waste. You deposit several different items. What is the mean cost per item to recycle?

Your car needs 1,250 gallons of gas to go 25,000 miles. You set aside the equivalent amount of money to convert your car to use renewable energy instead. How much money is this?

In 2002, the world's population was about 6,215,000,000. The population of the United States was 287,400,000. What percent of the world's population was the population of the United States?

You volunteer with an animal protection agency. The first turtle found in 2003 laying her eggs was discovered on April 9. If this is the only turtle who survives from the 162 hatchlings counted the year she was born, what is the percent survival rate?

What You Can Learn from This Unit

When you complete this unit, you will have used mathematics to work problems related to sustaining the world. These problems are similar to those that may actually occur in your daily life.

92

Example The recycle center charges different fees for depositing different types of waste. Chris and Amelia-Ann deposit two batteries, an old TV set, and a pile of paper. They also deposit a trash bag of aluminum cans and a load of brush. What is the mean cost for depositing these different types of waste?

Acme Recycle Center
Fee Schedule

Load of Brush	$3
Batteries	$1 per item
Household items:	$4 per item
Paper, plastic, aluminum:	free

Solve

Step 1: Add the cost of depositing all the items.

2 × $1 + $4 + $3 = $9

Step 2: Now count the number of different types of item.

batteries, household item, paper,   There are
aluminum, load of brush   5 types.

Step 3: Divide the total cost by the number of types of item.

$9 ÷ 5 = $1.80

Answer the Question

Step 4: The mean cost per type for their deposit at the recycle center is $1.80.

✐ Now try these problems.

1. The collection center charges $4 to deposit a load of miscellaneous waste. They charge $5 to deposit a large household item. They charge $3 to deposit any number of car or truck tires. They charge nothing to deposit paper, plastic, glass, or aluminum. Jake and Mora deposit an old refrigerator, a TV set, 4 old tires, and a pile of paper. What is the mean cost per type that they deposit at the recycle center?

   Answer: The mean cost per type is $_____.

2. The town receives a grant for $6,000 to collect and safely dispatch hazardous waste. The hazardous waste management company charges the town $7,500. Shade the diagram to show the portion of the cost that the grant represents.

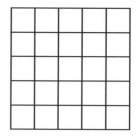

3. The skateboard club holds a fund-raiser to build more skateboard ramps. The club collects 45 gallons of old paint. They mix it together and offer it to the community. In exchange, the club asks for financial donations. Citizens take 36 gallons and donate $468. What is the mean donation per gallon for the gallons that the club gives away?

    A $10.10   **C** $60

    B $13   **D** $468

4. The art association asks the high school students to help collect trash off the beach. They want to build a "trash-to-treasures" sculpture as part of the annual beach festival. The students collect 3 truckloads of trash in 2.5 hours.

Circle the expression that tells how much trash, in truckloads, they collect per half hour?

$$3 \div 2.5 \qquad 3 \div 2.5 \div 2 \qquad 3 \times 2.5 \qquad 3 \times 2.5 \div 4$$

☆ Challenge Problem
You may want to talk this one over with a partner.

Your school decides to raise money by collecting cans, bottles, and paper to recycle. You post the figures that the trash collection company has promised you.

Recyclable Item	Price
Aluminum cans	$0.40 per pound
Number 1 plastic bottles	$0.06 each
White paper	$0.10 per pound

Write an expression that tells how much money you raise. Use c for the number of pounds of aluminum cans you collect. Use b for the number of plastic bottles. Use p for the number of pounds of white paper.

♜ A Board Game (for Two or More Players)

The goal of this game is to recover all the blacked-out areas. However, the game is over when the whole board is blacked out. First, you toss the number cubes to find the dimensions of a rectangular area. Then you black out that area, unless you tossed a double. Then you apply the doubles rules. Some doubles protect areas. Other doubles recover areas. One double blacks out the entire area! When you protect an area, you draw a heavy line around its perimeter.

Materials

Erasable game board (on the next page) or multiple paper copies of the board, pencils for shading, two number cubes.

Special doubles rules:

Double 1: Total black out. The game is over!

Double 2: Protect a 2 × 2 square for beautification. It uses renewable energy sources.

Double 3: Protect a seven-square **W** shape for wildlife protection. It uses no energy source.

Double 4: Protect a seven-square **H** shape for historic preservation. It is protected from blackout.

Double 5: Recover any two areas that share the same shape.

Double 6: Recover all blacked-out areas. Player (round winner) has solved energy problems.

Directions

1. Sit with players around the game board.
2. Player 1 tosses the two number cubes. If the toss is a double, refer to the special combination list and follow the directions. Otherwise, Player 1 chooses a rectangle described by the two numbers and shades it in which blacks it out. For example, the numbers 3 and 4 describe a rectangle of 3 squares by 4 squares. Player 1 can choose any 3 by 4 rectangle and shade it in.
3. Players then take turns doing the same thing. If a player tosses a number combination that is not available on the board, that player loses the turn. (This may be because some of the rectangle of that shape is already blacked out or protected.)
4. A round winner is a player who tosses double 6. All blacked-out areas are recovered. (Erase the shaded areas. Leave the protected areas.) The game continues. There can be as many round winners as you choose to continue the game.
5. The game is over when a player tosses a double 1 and everything is blacked out.

Game Board for *Black Out!*

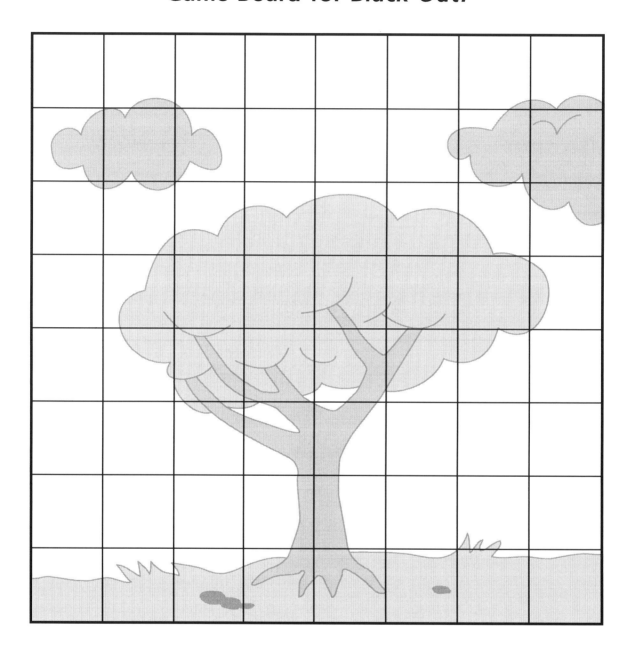

Lesson 3

Finding Other Ways

Example In the 1990s, the "Veggie Van" made a trip of 25,000 miles running on used vegetable oil from fast-food restaurants. The fuel cost nothing. Danny figures that *his* van needs 1,250 gallons of gas to go that far. Gas costs $1.60 a gallon. He sets aside that much money to convert his van to run on used vegetable oil. He looks forward to doing the same trip and breaking even. How much money does he set aside? What happens when he "breaks even"?

Solve

Step 1: Write a sentence in words to tell the total cost of gas for the trip.

The total cost of gas will be 1,250 gallons at $1.60 a gallon.

Step 2: Now write the same sentence, using the language of math.

Total cost of gas = 1,250 × $1.60
= $2,000

Step 3: Write a sentence that tells the amount of money Danny sets aside.

Danny sets aside the cost of gas for the trip. He sets aside $2,000.

Answer the Question

Step 4: Danny sets aside $2,000. Danny plans to spend this money to convert his van. He expects to spend nothing on fuel. When he breaks even, the cost for gas equals the cost of conversion. The trip costs him the same either way.

✏ Now try these problems.

1. Karli does about 10,000 miles a year in her car. She figures that her car needs 400 gallons of gas to go that far. Gas costs $1.75 a gallon. She cuts in half the miles she travels in a year. She sets aside her savings from fewer trips. She is going to use these savings to convert her car to run on solar energy. How much money does she set aside?

Answer: $_____

2. Joey is excited about installing clean-fuel equipment in his car. He has found out that he can get a tax credit of up to 50% of the cost of the project. If it costs him $2,800 to install the equipment, how much will his tax credit be worth? Fill in the information on the form.

Clean-fuel tax credit form	
Cost of installation project:	$2,800
Tax credit (at ____% of cost of project):	$_____

3. The county that Marissa lives in receives a grant. The grant is used to install a hot-water system that uses solar energy. The system is expected to save about $76,000 in annual energy costs. What is the mean savings per month?

A $633.33   **B** $760.00   **C** $7,600.00   **D** $6,333.33

4. Between 1989 and 1999, the overall consumption of renewable energy increased. Order these types of energy based on the percent they each changed. Put 1 in the column titled Order for the one with the highest percent increase. Number the other types in descending order of percent change from increase to decrease.

Type of energy	Btu's in 1989	Btu's in 1999	Order
Solar	0.059	0.076	
Wind	0.024	0.038	
Geothermal	0.338	0.327	
Wood and Waste	3.050	3.514	

☆ Challenge Problem
You may want to talk this one over with a partner.

Jason's family has a wind turbine that has rotors 25 feet in diameter. The turbine stands 30 feet high. It supplies the power needs of their all-electric home. The largest wind turbine has propellers that span more than the length of a football field. This largest turbine is located in Hawaii. It stands 20 building stories high. It produces enough electricity to power 1,400 homes. Are the heights of the two wind turbines in proportion to the power generated? If not, what do you think explains the difference?

_____

_____

_____

Lesson 4

The People of the World

Example In 2002, the world's population was about 6,215,000,000. This information is from the World Population Data Sheet. The population of the United States was 287,400,000. What percent of the world's population was the population of the United States?

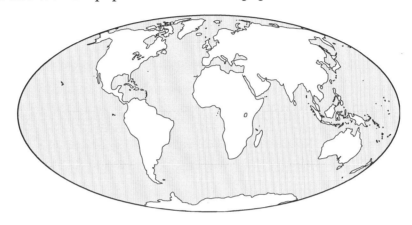

Solve

Step 1: The U.S. population is part of the world's population. You are going to compare these two as a percent. First, write the population of the United States as divided by the world's population.

287,400,000 ÷ 6,215,000,000 = 0.0462

Step 2: To write this decimal as a percent, multiply it by 100.

0.0462 × 100 = 4.62

Answer the Question

Step 4: The population of the United States was 4.62% of the world's population.

✎ Now try these problems.

1. In 2001, China ranked number 1 in population. Its population was 1,273,111,290. The United States ranked number 3. Its population was 278,058,881. What percent of the China's population was the population of the United States?

   A 2.18%   **C** 21.84%

   B 4.12%   **D** 41.23%

2. In 2002, more than 20% of the population of the United States was under 15 years of age. The population of the United States

was 287,400,000. The diagram represents 28.74 million people. One face stands for ten million people. Shade the faces that together represent the number of people under 15 years of age.

3. In a small Texas town, Suzanna encourages the community to get together to build a home for a needy family. The project takes 2 years, $15,000 cash and donated materials, and a total of 4,200 hours. About how much money and how many people-hours is that per month?

Answer: The project costs about $_____ and takes

_____ people-hours per month.

4. On Ashton's street, there is a family from each of 4 different continents. According to the International Organization of Migration, 150 million people live outside their countries of origin. The world's population is over 6.2 billion people. What percent of the world's population are those living outside their original country? Circle the best estimate.

2.0%   2.5%   3.0%   5.0%   20.0%   25.0%

☆ Challenge Problem
You may want to talk this one over with a partner.

In the 1970s, some forgotten writer said that 75% of people who have ever been born were now alive. If the statement was true, what conclusions can you draw from that fact?

_____

_____

_____

_____

100

Lesson 5

Success Stories of Species

Example According to scientists, more than 1.5 million species exist on Earth today. However, recent estimates state that at least 20 times that many species inhabit the planet. How much less is the previous scientific estimate than the more recent estimates?

Solve

Step 1: Write a sentence using math language to express the difference.

(20 × 1.5 million) − 1.5 million.

Step 2: Rewrite using the distributive property. The common factor becomes the multiplier in front of the parentheses.

1.5 million (20 − 1)

Step 3: Simplify the number in parentheses. Then multiply to find the answer.
1.5 million × 19 = 28.5 million

Answer the Question

Step 4: The previous scientific estimate is 28.5 million less than the recent estimates.

✏️ Now try these problems.

1. In the United States, 735 species of plants and 496 species of animals are listed as threatened or endangered. Of these, 266 species have recovery plans. How many of the total number of species do *not* have recovery plans?

Answer: The number of species without recovery plans is _____.

2. Nan volunteers with a turtle protection agency. She has a special interest in the endangered Kemp's ridley turtle. The first Kemp's ridley turtle nest laid in 2003 in the United States was found on April 9th. This turtle is one of 162 counted when they hatched in Mexico in 1993. If this is the only turtle that survives, what is the percent survival rate?

A 0.0062%   **B** 0.62%   **C** 1.62%   **D** 16.2%

3. There are more than 3,500 national parks and nature reserves worldwide. They occupy about 2 million square miles. Kim and James have volunteered at 15 different parks, monitoring wildlife. Based on the mean size of a park or reserve, about how many square miles of parks and reserves have they worked in? Fill in the blanks in the expression that tells the answer.

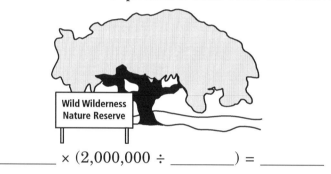

Wild Wilderness
Nature Reserve

_____ × (2,000,000 ÷ _____) = _____

4. Alison visits schools and nature groups to tell them about backyard habitats for wildlife. In three and a half years, she has helped 65 different groups to set up these habitats. What is the mean number of habitats per year that she has helped set up? Mark the number line at the point that comes closest to the mean number.

15.0   17.0   19.0   21.0
○ ○ ○ ○ ○ ○ ○ ○ ○ ○ ○ ○ ○

Challenge Problem
You may want to talk this one over with a partner.

At least 50% of the world species live in tropical forests. Okapis are found only in the tropical forests of northeast Zaire. They feed primarily on leaves, buds, and shoots of over 100 different species of forest vegetation. Estimates state that every hour at least 4,500 acres of tropical forest fall. What do you think are likely outcomes for the future of the Okapi?

_____

_____

_____

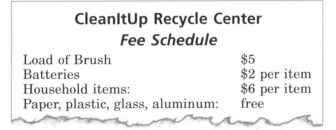

Unit 8 — Review

Review What You Learned

In this unit you have used mathematics to solve many problems. You have used mental math and estimation, practiced basic operations, and solved equations.

These two pages give you a chance to review the mathematics you used and check your skills.

✔ Check Your Skills

1. The recycle center charges different fees for depositing different types of waste. AnneMarie deposits a battery, an old couch, a box of glass bottles, and a load of brush. From the fee schedule, calculate the total cost and the mean cost per type.

> **CleanItUp Recycle Center**
> *Fee Schedule*
>
> Load of Brush $5
> Batteries $2 per item
> Household items: $6 per item
> Paper, plastic, glass, aluminum: free

Answer: The total cost is $_____ and the mean cost is $_____.
If you need to review, return to lesson 1 (page 93).

2. In the 1990s, the "Veggie Van" made a trip of 25,000 miles running on used vegetable oil. The fuel cost nothing. Danny figures that *his* van needs 1,000 gallons of gas to go that far. Gas costs $1.50 a gallon. He sets aside that much money to convert his van to run on used vegetable oil. How much money does he set aside? Choose the correct expression and fill in the blanks.

A 25,000 ÷ _____ × $1.50 = _____

B 1,000 × _____ = _____

C 25,000 − _____ ÷ _____ = $1,500

D $1.50 × _____ ÷ _____ = _____

If you need to review, return to lesson 3 (page 97).

3. From 1990 to 1999, the generation of geothermal, solar, wind, wood, and waste electric power increased by 98 billion kilowatt-hours. This was an average annual rate of 6.5%. The United

States, Japan, Germany, Brazil, and Finland accounted for 62% of the total. What is the mean percent per country?

Answer: _____

If you need to review, return to lesson 3 (page 97).

4. In 2001, China ranked number 1 in population. Its population was 1,273,111,290. India ranked number 2. Its population was 1,029,991,145. Shade the faces that represent the fraction that China's population was of India's population.

If you need to review, return to lesson 4 (page 99).

5. In a small town, Josh and Toby get the community together to build a home for a needy family. The project takes 1.5 years, $9,000 cash and donated materials, and 5,670 people-hours. About how much money and people is that per month? Fill in the calculations.

$9,000 ÷ _____ = _____   5,670 ÷ _____ = _____

If you need to review, return to lesson 4 (page 99).

6. According to scientists, more than 1.5 million species exist on Earth today. However, recent estimates state that at least 20 times that many species inhabit the planet. How much greater are the recent estimates than the previous scientific estimate?

    A 28.5 million   **C** 57 million

    B 30 million   **D** 28.5 billion

If you need to review, return to lesson 5 (page 101).

Write Your Own Problem ✍

Choose a problem you liked from this unit. Write a similar problem using a situation and related facts from your own life. With a partner, share and solve these problems together. Discuss the mathematics and compare the steps you used. If you need to, rewrite or correct the problems. Write your edited problem and the answer here.

_____

_____

_____

_____

To the Teacher

Welcome to *Everyday Life,* Book 1 of the *21st Century Lifeskills Mathematics* series.

Mastery of practical math skills is the overarching goal of the *21st Century Lifeskills Mathematics* series. To this end, each of the six books has been carefully designed to present topics students are likely to encounter in everyday life. Each book includes problems that involve estimation, equations, mental math, calculators, and critical thinking. Each book includes additional concept-specific skills such as graphing, averages, statistics, ratios, and measurement.

The books are appropriate for use with small groups, a full class, or by independent learners. The self-explanatory nature of the lessons frees the teacher for individual instruction. Each unit begins with a preview lesson, which models and explains the types of problems students will encounter in the unit. Then there are five lessons, at least one of which is a game. Game titles are italicized in the Table of Contents, on the lesson pages, and in the Answer Key. Each unit ends with a review of the unit concepts. Both illustrations and graphic art are used to support the instruction and maintain interest. A variety of problem types and games are used to sharpen critical thinking skills throughout the program.

Below are the titles of the other books in the *21st Century Lifeskills Mathematics* series:

Book 2: Home & School
Book 3: On the Job
Book 4: Budgeting & Banking
Book 5: Smart Shopping
Book 6: Sports, Hobbies, & Recreation

Students from middle school through adult classes will appreciate the practical content of each book.

Through modeling, practice, and review, students will build their math skills and learn to approach everyday mathematical situations with confidence. *21st Century Lifeskills Mathematics* will help your students become successful problem solvers!

Unit 1: Personal Care

Lesson 1: Hair Care

1. $40.00
2. D 700
3. Draw line between 7 ounces and $9.99
4. 4 weeks
5. $10 bill
6. B $1

Challenge Problem. No, because it will only have grown 4 inches.

Lesson 2: Face & Skin Care

1. 1,003
2. 2 gift boxes circled
3. Lotion, dry skin kit, and face scrub
4. C $780

Lesson 3: *Soapy Percents*

1. three spaces that show 50%
2. 3, 5

Lesson 4: Dental Care

1. $200
2. C $720
3. Parsley is the cheaper way to freshen your breath, by 24.5 cents a week.
4. $77 is circled; $4.62 has a square around it; $11 is in the blank.

Challenge Problem. Both are the same: 10% of 8% of product price is the same as 8% of 10% of product price.

Lesson 5: Accessories

1. $217.75
2. C $375
3. The last row should be circled, showing No and No.
4. $617.50

Challenge Problem. Answers may vary. Sample answer: The total value of all purchases that are less than $50 each.

Review

1. $20.50
2. 1,260
3. 60%
4. $\frac{4}{10}$ or $\frac{2}{5}$
5. $315
6. A $232.65

Unit 2: Health

Lesson 1: Nutrition

1. 300 g
2. C 0.72 mg
3. fill in chart
4. **a.** 1/2,400; **b.** 99.95%

Challenge Problem. 735 children

Lesson 2: *Calories Count*

1. 1,625 grams
2. $\frac{1}{4}$

Lesson 3: Medication

1. 17 days
2. 2 × 3 = 6
3. B 3
4. John should take 9 capsules over 4 days.

Challenge Problem. Sample response: Yes. Over 50% were helped with the new medicine, while only 10% said there was an improvement with the placebo.

Lesson 4: Getting Exercise, Staying Fit

1. 4
2. 144
3. C 412.50
4. Curtis, by 3 laps
5. 6 hours

Challenge Problem. Sample response: He needs to know how long each of the four steps (2 through 5) will take him.

Lesson 5: Vitamin Power

1. 75
2. $1\frac{1}{3}$ servings
3. Package of salmon chowder

4. Divide the total number of raisins in the box by three (Beverly and her two friends).

Challenge Problem. Hal is right. Explanation should support the answer.

Review

1. 8 g
2. B 6
3. 33
4. No, she is not correct. The difference is 1.0 calories/hour/kilogram (12.6 − 11.6).
5. 6

Unit 3: Getting Around

Lesson 1: Bus Schedules

1. 10:00 a.m.
2. D every 2 hours
3. 10:10 a.m.
4. 3:45 p.m.
5. 3 hours

Challenge Problem. The earliest they can get back to the town center is 4:30 p.m. Their parking fee is $3.75.

Lesson 2: Bicycles

1. Wheel Revolutions: 3.2; 6.4; 12.8; 16
2. A 12
3. 125 revolutions; 10,125 inches; 843.75 feet
4. 168.75 feet

Challenge Problem. **a.** 708.3 feet; **b.** 745.4 revolutions; 9.44 minutes

Lesson 3: Walking

1. 7
2. The first column is circled ($\frac{1}{2}$; 1; 3).
3. C 6 miles
4. 10

Challenge Problem. Yes, if all bridges are intact. No, if bridge X collapses.

Unit 3 *(continued)*

Lesson 4: *Maps & Directions*
1. A 6 miles east, 13 miles south
2. 32.5

Lesson 5: Traveling by Car
1. Second row is circled: 55 mph; $109.38; 35 hours.
2. **a.** 160 miles; **b.** 53.33 miles per hour
3. **a.** less; **b.** lower; **c.** more; **d.** more
4. D 70 mph

Challenge Problem. Sample answer: Two other routes are modifications of the route shown. A route can only extend two grid points to the east. Explanations should support the answer.

Starting Point

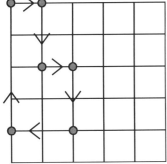

Review
1. C 12 noon
2. 200 revolutions
3. X
4. 5:25 p.m.
5. NE
6. **a.** 9.3 gallons; **b.** 7.8 hours

Unit 4: Managing Time

Lesson 1: Sleep
1. 90
2. +
3. 5 hours
4. B 2,016
5. **a.** –3; **b.** –6; **c.** +6

Challenge Problem. n → 5n → 5n + 4 → 10n + 8 → 10n → 10

Lesson 2: Time Zones
1. C 9 p.m.
2. the states in the Central time zone
3. They have gained 2 hours.
4. Change the time to 5 p.m.
5. D 8 p.m.

Challenge Problem. There are only 2 possible sequences: 2,4,1,3 and 3,1,4,2.

Lesson 3: *The Small-Black-Circle Game*
1. equilateral triangle, circle, square, or pentagon, each large or small and black, gray, or white
2. triangular; at one corner

Lesson 4: Cycles of Time
1. May 2, 3, 9, and 10
2. D 29
3. 2005; 2011
4. 12 different council members

Challenge Problem. Technologies that are not developed yet; explanation should support answer.

Lesson 5: Spending Time
1. Yes, they met their goal. $\frac{3}{4}$ of the clock face is shaded.
2. **a.** 20%; **b.** 2.08
3. D $13
4. (54 − 45) ÷ 45 = 20%
5. The first expression is circled.

Challenge Problem. 1 hour. If the time were 12:30 p.m. or 1 p.m., he would have to wait for the next two sets of strikes.

Review
1. 7:45 a.m.
2. 0.45 × 2,000
3. D 10 p.m.
4. 2005
5. 38%

Unit 5: Community

Lesson 1: Education
1. 9 credit hours
2. C less than
3. Student should circle the invoice that reads "$88 per credit hour."
4. **a.** $295 (Circle all the fees, except tuition, in the row for 9 credit hours.); **b.** $780

Challenge Problem. The health and advisor fees do not increase as the number of credit hours increases. The student service fee does not increase after 12 credit hours. The numerator (fees) is not increasing as fast as the denominator (credit hours).

Lesson 2: Post Office
1. **a.** Sample answer: ($4.40 + $1.00 + $5.50) = $10.90; **b.** Sample answer: 55 cents
2. B 19
3. Sample answers: 0 dollar bill; 2 quarters; 0 dimes; 0 nickels; 2 pennies
4. $a / 2 + 1$

Challenge Problem. You will pick up your mail on Wednesday, May 14.

Lesson 3: Library
1. The mean number of days Trey has to read each of the other books is 3 days.
2. Fill in rows as follows: 2 books: 0.50; 1.00; 1.50; 2.00; 2.50; 3.00; 3.50; 3 books: .075; 1.50; 2.25; 3.00; 3.75; 4.50; 5.25; 4 books: 1.00; 2.00; 3.00; 4.00; 5.00; 6.00; 7.00.
3. 6; 3; 2; 1
4. D $48

Challenge Problem. $13.35. Sample answer: You need to know the number of books that were late and the fine per book per day.

Lesson 4: A Passport to Travel
1. 20
2. B 25 years old
3. $x = 1.08$; $y = 4$
4. any combination of bills that adds to $115
5. 2 weeks and 0 days

Unit 5 (continued)

Challenge Problem. The results can be only these ten numbers: 0, 99, 198, 297, 396, 495, 594, 693, 792, 891. Sample response: The digits are *x, y,* and *z.* So the difference between the numbers is $100x + 10y + z - (100z + 10y + x)$ equals $99x - 99y$ or $99(x - y)$. The value of *y* can be 0 to 9; the value of *x* can be 1 to 9 so $(x - y)$ can be 0, 1, 2, 3, 4, 5, 6, 7, 8, or 9. Multiply each of these values by 99 to get all the possibilities for the difference of the two 3-digit numbers.

Lesson 5: *Government Services*

1. $1,025
2. $165

Review

1. 12
2. On the second invoice, answer written in is a reasonable number greater than $95.
3. B $13.50
4. Circle Friday the twenty-second.
5. 28

Unit 6: Thinking about the Future

Lesson 1: Career Options

1. $29,849; $54,191.80; $43,140; $40,114
2. C $2,250
3. Lines are drawn between $46,690 and 70%; $3,335 and 5%; $2,668 and 4%; $1,334 and 2%; $6,003 and 9%; $2,001 and 3%; $4,669 and 7%.

Challenge Problem. Explanations should support choices and include the fact that cost of living and merit can vary.

Lesson 2: Costs of Living

1. $16 + 1 \times s = 52 \times 2$, so $s = 88$. She can spend $88.
2. a mean cost of $377 per month
3. D $126
4. $41

Challenge Problem. Starting at the top of the triangle and proceeding clockwise the numbers are 9, 4, 3, 7, 6, 2, 8, 5, 1.

Lesson 3: *Making Money*

1. $195
2. $1,000,000

Lesson 4: Paying Taxes

1. $8,168.75
2. Fitness club membership
3. Change the figure to $1,050.
4. D $1,113

Challenge Problem. At least $752.40; $8276.40 plus next year's taxes. Opinions will vary but should be supported with reasons.

Lesson 5: Getting Insurance

1. Judith pays $172 more than Mindy.
2. $150
3. $95 - 75 = 20$
4. C $1,000,000

Challenge Problem. Sample response: J. L. takes out disability insurance to make sure he will continue to earn a reasonable salary even if he becomes disabled and can no longer play. The team takes out insurance to ensure the income they expect to make as a result of J. L. being on the team.

Review

1. $13,916
2. $2,463 ÷ 6 = $410.50
3. $249.15
4. C $5666.25
5. $1,367

Unit 7: Thrifty Thinking

Lesson 1: *Sales & Bargains— Shop 'Til You Drop!*

1. A He spends $30 and saves $10.

Lesson 2: Do It Yourself

1. $1.80; 20 minutes; $1.86
2. Supplies $12.50; Labor $70.00; Total cost $178.50; Answer $71.50

3. They save $10. Responses may mention the pleasure and satisfaction of doing it themselves.

Challenge Problem. Responses may mention the cost of food handling equipment, plates and cutlery, people's time to man the booth, and food handler's licenses.

Lesson 3: Buying in Bulk

1. $0.55; $1.24
2. A $93.75
3. Circle under Expenses 1,000 × $4.50; Income 1,000 × $7; Profit 1,000 × $2.50

Challenge Problem. Responses may mention that the moving company will probably be cheaper than the office supply company but more expensive than the (free) supermarket.

Lesson 4: New versus Used

1. $105.23; $5.00 Reasons should include the sharply reduced cost of used clothing items.
2. 14 × ($0.89 - $0.30)
3. D mean: $10.63; mode: $17
4. $75

Challenge Problem. Responses might include these points: James' unit costs him $152 a year. Tony's unit costs him $100 a year. James does not have to replace his for 5 years. Tony has to replace his in 2 years.

Lesson 5: Conserving Resources

1. $6.60
2. Responses may mention that, over the long term, maintaining the same temperature may cost less than raising the temperature a significant number of degrees.
3. $4.60; $12.95; $3.70

Challenge Problem. Responses may point out that Gary saves time waiting in line to put his car on the ferry and saves gas doing short trips. He also gets exercise biking

Unit 7 *(continued)*

to work. However, he cannot make long trips or carry large packages on his bicycle.

Review

1. $7.50; $22.50; $22.50; $7.50
2. C $5; $3
3. 275 + 2 × 4 × 5 × 8
4. $2.50 − ($12 ÷ 10) = $1.30
5. $2.37

Unit 8: Sustaining the World

Lesson 1: Recovering Waste

1. $4.33
2. All but final column of squares is shaded. (20 squares shaded; 5 are not shaded.)
3. B $13
4. 3 ÷ 2.5 ÷ 2

Challenge Problem. $c × 0.40 + b × 0.06 + p × 0.10$

Lesson 2: *Black Out!*

There are no answers in this game. The game is over when a player tosses a double 1 and everything is blacked out.

Lesson 3: Finding Other Ways

1. $350
2. 50%; $1,400
3. D 6,333.33
4. Fill in order column with the following: 2, 1, 4, 3

Challenge Problem. The heights are not in proportion to the power generated. Possible explanation lies in the difference in the rotor size and average wind strength.

Lesson 4: The People of the World

1. C 21.84%
2. 5.75 of the faces are shaded.
3. $625; 175
4. 2.5%

Challenge Problem. Responses may mention that the number of births in the twentieth century would have to have been far, far greater than in the whole rest of human history. The population growth of the world was very slow for a long time and has increased rapidly in recent years.

Lesson 5: Success Stories of Species

1. 965
2. B 0.62%
3. 15 × (2,000,000 ÷ 3,500) = 8,571.43
4. The circle below the 18.5 mark on the line is darkened.

Challenge Problem. Sample answer: If tropical forests fall, vegetation goes with them. If this is the vegetation that Okapis feed on, in time they will die out.

Review

1. $13; $3.25
2. B 1,000 × $1.50 = $1,500
3. 12.4%
4. 9.75 faces should be shaded.
5. $9,000 ÷ 18 = $500; 5,670 ÷ 18 = 315
6. A 28.5 million